MORAL PSYCHOLOGY

CONNOR WHITELEY

No part of this book may be reproduced in any form or by any electronic or mechanical means. Including information storage, and retrieval systems, without written permission from the author except for the use of brief quotations in a book review.

This book is NOT legal, professional, medical, financial or any type of official advice.

Any questions about the book, rights licensing, or to contact the author, please email connorwhiteley@connorwhiteley.net

Copyright © 2024 CONNOR WHITELEY

All rights reserved.

DEDICATION
Thank you to all my readers without you I couldn't do what I love.

INTRODUCTION

Why do people do good and bad things?

Whilst psychology generally focuses on the empirical study of human behaviour, I have to admit this covers a lot of ground. For example, how our social groups impact us, how different environmental and social factors impact our mental health, and how children develop.

Psychology covers a lot of different facets of human behaviour.

However, moral psychology, which is a subfield of social psychology, focuses on why humans do "good or moral" behaviours and "bad or immoral" behaviours in a given situation. This is even more interesting when we consider there are universal moral behaviours, like don't kill and loving your children, and universal immoral behaviours, like abuse and killing innocent people.

Yet there are moral grey areas too.

Therefore, in this book, you'll be learning a lot about the social psychology of morality by looking at different studies, theories and practical examples that I add into the book to help you understand the sheer complexity and fascinating nature of morality.

How Is This Book Structured?

I know morality is a very large and complex area of psychology, so I want to stress this book will be structured in an engaging and easy-to-understand way. Hence, the book will be divided up into the following four sections:

- Part One focuses on introducing you to morality by talking about some basic theories, principles and criticisms within the field so you can understand the basics of moral psychology.
- Part Two focuses on the wide range of social factors influencing our morality and moral judgement. For instance, our relationships with different people, social influence, authority figures and much more.
- Part Three focuses on moral grey areas and the social psychological theories and mechanisms that explain why people commit morally grey acts.
- Part Four focuses on morality in the real-world and the consequences of morality.

Overall, there are a lot of fun, engaging and fascinating facets of moral psychology explored in this book and all the information is explained and written in my characteristic engaging and conversational tone. Despite being fact- and evidence-based, this isn't like a boring university textbook. This is a psychology book you actually want to read.

Who Am I?

Personally, I always love to know who the author is of the nonfiction I read so I know the information is coming from a good source. In case you're like me, I'm Connor Whiteley, the internationally bestselling author of over 40 psychology books.

In addition, I am the host of *The Psychology World Podcast,* a weekly show exploring a new psychology topic each week and delivering the latest psychology news. Available on all major podcast apps and YouTube.

Finally, I am a psychology graduate studying a Clinical Psychology Masters at the University of Kent, England until September 2025.

So now we know more about each other, let's dive into the great topic of moral psychology.

PART ONE: INTRODUCTION TO MORALITY AND MORAL PSYCHOLOGY

MORAL PSYCHOLOGY

INTRODUCTION TO MORAL REASONING, MORAL JUDGEMENTS AND MORAL FOUNDATIONS THEORY

To kick off this massive topic, I wanted to start us off by focusing on moral reasoning a little and a lot of the information in this chapter, we'll expand out over the rest of the book as well as add to. Yet we need to start somewhere and when it comes to dealing with why people do right and wrong, we need to start with the basics.

And emotions can certainly be basic (and everyone who has ever read *Cognitive Psychology* is laughing).

Anyway, emotions are a great place to start because emotions are important in guiding our moral judgements.

A rather brilliant example of emotions and moral judgements can be found in Haidt (2001) who got university students to read a story about a brother and sister who had sex using birth control.

This was a great stimulus to show people because it triggers a lot of great emotions in people and it definitely triggers disgust.

As a result, university students immediately said that the siblings having sex was wrong when they experienced disgust. Yet what was really interesting was the participants couldn't explain why or how they had come to make their moral judgement.

Instead the participants simply said "incest was just wrong" or inbreeding was wrong for genetic reasons. That's an argument I understand because it is true, but it is a useless argument in this situation because birth control was used. Making the genetic argument null-void.

Therefore, Haidt argued that moral reasoning is based on emotion and gut-feelings about what is right and wrong (Greene & Haidt, 2002; Haidt, 2003). Since the participants "just knew" that incest was wrong but they couldn't explain their reasoning, because the emotional response of disgust probably guided moral judgements about the situation.

Personally, I agree with the results because I was still disgusted when I first read about a brother and sister having sex. I couldn't explain why. I think I was disgusted by it because society has told me incest is wrong, and I support the genetic argument.

But is that objectively enough of a reason to make a moral judgement?

No, so the research supports the argument that emotion plays a role in moral judgements.

<u>Emotions Guiding Moral Behaviour</u>

Furthermore, emotions don't only guide our moral judgements because they play a role in our moral behaviours too, so the moral and immoral actions we perform.

The two most studied emotions in this regard are shame and guilt, because these are associated with immoral actions. As well as people are more likely to want to make up for immoral actions when experiencing these emotions (Tangey, Miller, Flicker & Barlow, 1996; Tangney, Wagner, Hill-Barlow, Marschall & Gramzow, 1996).

Although, it is worth noting that shame and guilt aren't the same thing. Due to when someone is experiencing shame, they're more concerned with how they are being seen by other people so this is associated with an externalisation of blame.

Whereas guilt is the opposite because if I feel guilt then I'm feeling bad because I have personally acted in an immoral way.

As a result, if we apply these findings to the real-world then it shouldn't be too much of a surprise to learn that shame-prone criminal offenders compared to guilt-prone offenders appear to be more likely to reoffend (Tangney et al., 2014).

I don't think this is too surprising because I know from clinical psychology that people only change their behaviour if they have a motivation. In therapy, this is a motivation to decrease their psychological distress, improve their life and want to develop more adaptive (better) coping mechanisms.

Yet in criminal reoffending, if you don't feel like you're to blame and you don't feel negatively about this blame, then you have no motivation to change. Hence, the increased risk of reoffending.

In addition, different emotions are experienced in different moral domains. Since people tend to feel more anger when others violate morals about the freedom and rights of others (Rozin et al., 1999; Vasquez et al. 2011). Whereas people experience disgust more when people violate morals regarding the purity of a person's character, body and mind (Haidt et al., 1993; Rozin et al., 1999).

I would like to add that the idea of "purity" is a good example of social norms and constructs, an argument we'll explore later on so keep a pin in that.

Moral Signalling

Another function of communicating our moral judgements is twofold. We can communicate our intense moral disapproval to other people and we can use this to signal our own moral character (Kupfer & Giner-Sorolla, 2017; Giner-Sorolla, Kupfer & Sabo, 2018).

Which can have social benefits for us. For example, it can make us feel good because we can say we are a more moral (and "better" person) than them. As well as we can show our friends we're a better person which always makes us feel good.

Overall, the emotions of disgust and anger might be expressed differently in response to the violation of different moral principles.

Moral Foundations Theory

Our final theory for this chapter is a rather interesting one because on paper, it sounds great but I'll point out a few problems near the end of the chapter.

Moral Foundations Theory was proposed by Graham, Haidt & Nosek (2009) and Graham et al. (2013) being influenced by the work of Schweder et al. (1997).

The theory proposes there are five key moral foundations that we use to judge a person's behaviours.

- Purity- we should observe the sanctity or purity of the body and divine.

- Authority- people should respect and obey authority figures and leaders.

- Ingroup loyalty- people should be loyal to other people in our social group.

- Fairness- people should treat others fairly and with equality.

- Harm and care- people should care for other people and prevent harm from coming to them. This is especially true for the weak and most vulnerable in society.

Moreover, the theory says that Harm and Care as well as Fairness factors are individualising moral foundations because they're about the rights and welfare of an individual person. Whereas ingroup loyalty, authority and purity are seen as binding moral foundations because they're connected to the interests and values of a society. Yet this distinction has been criticised by Janoff-Bulman and Carnes (2013).

In addition, Graham et al. (2009) argued and showed with evidence that political liberals were more concerned with the rights and welfare of individuals than the traditional fabric of society. As well as Liberals would be especially concerned with the individualising foundations of harm and fairness, and less concerned about the violations of ingroup loyalty, purity and authority.

In terms of criticism, Moral Foundations Theory has been heavily criticised as an explanation for moral reasoning, as well as Graham et al. (2009)'s methodology has been targeted too.

Since Kugler et al. (2014) question whether loyalty to the ingroup, authority and to the divine should be regarded as moral at all.

This criticism gets very interesting when we start to think about real-world applications and examples. For example, to use a slightly political example, let's use the example of a politician resigning over their party's anti-environmental policies when they were the UK's former Energy Minister. Technically, this is disloyalty to the ingroup because this person was very public about why they were resigning.

So you could argue this is immoral behaviour

because this person is going against the ingroup of their political party. Yet this could be deemed moral behaviour because this person was standing up for what was right. Or this has nothing to do with morality at all, because this is just a person resigning as a protest and this isn't about whether this resignation and by extension separating from the ingroup is right or wrong.

This is what's so interesting about morality. There is no one answer but there are empirical findings that help to guide our knowledge.

Also, Kugler et al. (2014) found the relationship between political orientation and moral foundations was actually fully explained by right-wing authoritarianism instead of morality.

This is a very heavy finding against Moral Foundation Theory because it shows these five factors aren't looking at anything new. Instead they are simply looking at constructs already studied in social psychology just with some new fancy names.

Furthermore, Janoff-Bulman and Carnes (2013) criticised the suggestion that harm and fairness are individualising foundations that are only concerned with the individual. They can refer to harm and fairness done to groups too at a society-level group.

One such example that springs into my head is the historical (and still present but just in a different form) abuse against black and ethnic communities. Harm and a lack of fairness was committed against the entire group on a societal-level.

Similarly, authority, loyalty and subjective codes of purity can be as divisive as they are binding in any society that is made up of more than one group. Therefore, if this actually was a moral foundation that all human moral judgements are evaluated against. Then why is this so divisive and not binding?

Because it isn't a moral foundation.

On the whole, as imperfect as this Theory is, we have to admit it has generated a lot of research and received a lot of empirical support over the years. Like, Hofmann et al. (2014) found when participants reported moral and immoral acts they had seen on their smartphone, their reports fitted well with Moral Foundations Theory. Including how liberals and conservatives focus on different moral foundations.

Types Of Moral Thinking

To wrap up this first introductory chapter, I want to mention how psychology doesn't only look to itself when it comes to moral psychology, it can draw on philosophy too.

Therefore, there is a lot of talk within psychology of different types of moral thinking. This is what we'll focus on in this short section, because some of the results are surprising.

Firstly, you have utilitarianism moral thinking which is where the morality of the action is determined by how much benefit and harm the action does. Consequently, the acts are deemed moral if they have a good cost-benefit ratio.

Whereas consequentialist moral thinking is where

an action's morality depends on how they conform to moral rules that are applied regardless of the situation. Like "Though shalt not kill".

From a consequentialist viewpoint, it is flat out wrong to kill anyone regardless of whether they're an attacker, a rapist or someone is killed in self-defence.

According to philosophical and some other thinkers, people use one of the two types of moral decision-making. Yet in reality, research shows people typically use a mixture of these principles by weighing up the consequences of an action against the rules it might follow or break (Conway & Gawronski, 2013; Gawronski et al., 2017).

Although, people can find themselves in a dilemma at times when doing the right thing according to deontological rules also means doing harm.

Which is where the trolley problem comes in.

In case you're managed to study psychology or showed an interest in human behaviour without coming across the trolley problem (please tell me how you achieved that). The trolley problem is a moral dilemma where you are given the choice of interfering or doing nothing to stop a runaway trolley from killing five people.

This dilemma makes it useful in studying a range of behaviours (including the effects of hormones on behaviour from *Biological Psychology*) so it's been used in a lot of psychology studies in different variations.

Although, the reason why I'm mentioning it is

because research shows that most people prefer *not* to act so they choose the option that kills the most people. This is because people prefer not to break a moral rule about not killing anyone and this lack of breaking moral rules makes someone seem more moral to observers (Bostyn & Roets, 2017; Brown & Sacco, 2019; Everett et al., 2016; Sacco et al., 2017).

The reason why this doesn't break a moral rule is because whilst the person didn't do anything to stop the killing of the five people, they didn't do anything at all. Therefore, they can tell themselves the deaths aren't their fault and they didn't kill anyone.

Even if their actions meant more people died in the end.

Yet observers are more empathetic towards people who pull the lever (Gleichgerrcht & Young, 2013).

Now we understand moral judgements, moral reasoning and Moral Foundations Theory, let's continue our introduction to morality by looking at theories and principles of morality.

That's going to be a fun topic for sure.

PRINCIPLES AND THEORIES OF MORALITY

Before the creation of this book, this chapter served as the only "true" reference I had made to morality in all my books. There were of course other references or morality comments made in other chapters in other books but this is the only chapter that focuses on morality.

As a result, whilst this chapter has remained largely unchanged from its debut in *Developmental Psychology*, there have been updates, structural changes and more detail added in certain sections.

So let's continue our introduction to moral psychology and why people do what they do.

<u>Principles And Theories of Morality</u>

As a society and as humans, we like to think we exist by a moral code that protects us from doing harm to ourselves and others. But how does morality develop and what underpins morality? That's the focus for this chapter.

Personally, I think morality is vital to us as a social group because morality does act as a protective factor against us doing 'wrong' things and breaking social norms.

Also, morality and the concept of justice is made up of the following four principles:

- It's intuitive (gut-feelings)
- Moral thinking is for social driving (Social Cognition- I'll introduce this topic more in a moment)
- Morality binds and builds
- Morality is more than harm and fairness.

Over the course of the chapter, we'll look at each principle to see how accurate it really is. Except the final principle because this was examined in the last chapter with Moral Foundations Theory and its criticisms.

Social Cognition

As I mentioned earlier, the majority of this chapter originally came from my book *Developmental Psychology*, and in that book I explain what is and how Social Cognition develops. Yet I realised there might be readers new to social cognition reading this book, so I wanted to briefly explain what it is and why it is important to our survival.

Therefore, social cognition looks at the mental processes behind our social interactions and group processes.

These social processes are helped by primates having unusually large brains for our body size, and this comes with the price of very high energy costs. Meaning that to compensate for this high energy costs, there must be a good explanation for why we have this large organ that costs us so much energy.

This is where social cognition comes in.

Evolutionary:

Our social cognition can be explained by evolutionary theory because our large brains aided our survival as they allowed us to develop social skills. That allowed us to form groups and communities that was beneficial for the survival of the species. As this allowed us to hunt in packs, share the workload and aid in the survival of the species in other ways.

Ecological Hypothesis:

This hypothesis looks at the reason for our big brains from an environmental standpoint and the hypothesis proposes that our big brains are a bi-product of cognitive demands of certain behaviours. Like: foraging, mental maps of the landscape (for example), innovation and tool use.

As a result, these instrumental skills gave us a direct advantage over living as individuals for survival.

Therefore, we developed better foraging skills amongst other skills as we could forage in groups and learn from others.

Social Learning:

Personally, I have always loved social learning

theory as it's always useful and interesting to consider.

Therefore, applying social learning theory to Social Cognition, our large brains reflect the social skills that developed through social competition, and in order to achieve success socially, we needed to develop skills. Such as deception, forming alliances and manipulation.

Meaning that social skills gave a direct advantage to the individual to survive.

Thus, having and being able to use social skills is beneficial to the individual and not only the species.

And if you want to explore Social Cognition in more depth, please check out *Cognitive Psychology*, available wherever you got this book from.

<u>Principle 1:</u>

In an effort to explain the development of morality and how it's intuitive. We'll going to look at Kohlberg's theory of Moral Development. This is based on Piaget's theory of cognitive development as seen in Developmental Psychology. It proposes people go through consequential stages of moral development.

Kohlberg (1984) developed the theory by interviewing 72 Chicago boys aged 10–16 years and conducting follow-up interviews with 58 of them at three-yearly intervals for 20 years.

We can already tell from just the research sample that this is already going to be a study to critique. Since how can you propose universal rules of human behaviour with only males from one city in one country one continent? You can't.

The interviews were based on 2-hour interviews where the participants were presented with different moral dilemmas.

Here's an extract of one of the moral reasoning tasks:

"Heinz's wife was dying from a particular type of cancer. Doctors said a new drug might save her. The drug had been discovered by a local chemist, and the Heinz tried desperately to buy some, but the chemist was charging ten times the money it cost to make the drug, and this was much more than the Heinz could afford.

Heinz could only raise half the money, even after help from family and friends. He explained to the chemist that his wife was dying and asked if he could have the drug cheaper or pay the rest of the money later.

The chemist refused, saying that he had discovered the drug and was going to make money from it. The husband was desperate to save his wife, so later that night he broke into the chemist's and stole the drug."

Personally, I think this is a difficult task because yes he broke the law and social norms by stealing. But he did it for a good reason, to save the person he loved. Arguably this counts as protecting your family and loving your wife until death do them part. Both of these things are considered social norms. So, did he commit a moral or immoral act?

Anyway, this allowed Kohlberg to identify three distinct levels of moral reasoning within different stages of cognitive development. As well as he suggested that people can only pass through these levels in a certain order with each new stage replacing the reasoning typical of the earlier stage.

<u>Levels:</u>

The first level is at the Pre-Conventional level at the Obedience/Punishment Stage. Here the person focuses on avoiding punishment as well as the person doesn't see the difference between doing the right thing and avoiding punishment. As you probably guess this stage happens in infancy.

Secondly, you have the next stage at the same level but the Self-Interest Stage that happens in the pre-schooling years. In this stage, the person's moral behaviour starts to shift their focus to rewards over punishment and the focus is on getting the most benefits for ourselves.

The next stage in moral development happens at the Conventional Level with the Conformity Stage at school age. Which focuses on getting the approval of others and maintaining friendly relationships with others.

Subsequently, at the same time Conventional Level, you have the Law and Social Order Stage again this occurs during school years. At this age, the person focuses on fixed rules and the purpose of morality is seen as maintaining social order.

You see at this stage, the idea of morality starts

to become more complex and the person acts to be moral to maintain the social order.

The penultimate stage occurs at another level with the second to last stage happening at the Post-Conventional Level at Social Contract Orientation Stage during adolescence. Here the focus of morality is on achieving mutual benefits and rules that benefit everyone as well as people start to recognize that legality and morality isn't always the same thing. For example, you might think it's moral to commit euthanasia for a terminally ill person who is always in agony. But that's far from legal.

Finally, there's the Post-Conventional Level, Universal Human Ethic Stage that occurs around adulthood. Here the idea of morality is fully formed where people realise morality is based on principles that transcend mutual benefits. Since acting morally can cost us sometimes.

In my opinion, I think the theory is good overall as it clearly shows the developmental pathway for morality. And if we think about it, it does seem logical and it's good it builds on Piaget's theory.

However, the theory is not perfect.

Issues with Kohlberg's Theory

So, the first problem is are these stages really different and sequential? Due to people often fall back to different stages of the model depending on the moral dilemmas. Since reasoning about right and wrong depends on the situation more than some general rules.

Also, this theory is mainly based on the idea that morality is about justice and doing what is right. Compared to other factors that influence human behaviour. As showed by Gilligan (1978) who criticised Kohlberg on feminist psychology grounds. They argued that the principle of caring for others is equally as important as justice and there is a gender bias in the theory.

This point definitely questions the theory.

The final issue with the theory is, is moral psychology mostly about *reasoning*? As explained by this quote:

"We are claiming . . . that the moral force in personality is cognitive. Affective forces are involved in moral decisions, but affect is neither moral nor immoral. When the affective arousal is channeled into moral directions, it is moral; when it is not so channeled, it is not. The moral channeling mechanisms themselves are cognitive" (Kohlberg, 1971, pp. 230-231)

In my opinion, I disagree with this point slightly because emotions are involved in our thoughts and reasoning as I explain in Cognitive Psychology. So, not only are these influencing our reasoning but I think they do link to morality. Since if we take the trolley problem, pushing someone off a bridge to save five people is meant to be moral. But if someone pushed someone they hated and they were filled with satisfaction. Would they still be moral?

The theory says to only count on the reasoning.

So, this theory says they would be moral?

What would you say?

Haidt's Social Intuitionist Model

Continuing with our look at the first principle and how morality is linked to intuition. Haidt explains this link perfectly because he said: "Moral reasoning, when it occurs, is usually a post-hoc process in which we search for evidence to support our initial intuitive reaction". Haidt (2008)

Therefore, Haidt argues that people don't think about morality when it happens because it's our intuition.

As a result, we can find evidence for the social intuitionist model from four lines of inquiry and their findings. For example, people have near-instant implicit reactions to scenes and stories of situations that violate moral standards. (Luo et al, 2006) Supporting the idea of morality isn't about reasoning, it's immediate intuition.

In addition, a person's emotional reactions are usually good predictors of their moral judgments and behaviours (Sanfey et al, 2003)

Another piece of support is that if we manipulate a person's emotional reactions, like through hypnosis, we can change their moral judgments (Wheatley & Haidt, 2005) As well as people can sometimes be" morally dumbfounded" This happens when a person knows intuitively that something is wrong even when they cannot explain why (Haidt, 2001)

Furthermore, Damasio (1994) provides further

support for the model with the concept of "Acquired Sociopathy". This is an interesting example of morality because this occurs in patients with damage to certain areas of the prefrontal cortex but these people retained their cognitive abilities. Such as their IQ and their explicit knowledge of right and wrong. Suggesting their reasoning skills would be normal.

However, these patients showed massive emotional deficits, and these deficits greatly inhibited their judgment and decision-making. As well as patients with vmPFC damage tend to give normal responses to questions about how various hypothetical choices should be resolved, including various moral dilemmas (Saver & Damasio, 1991), but they struggle to make decisions about what to do with themselves in a *particular situation* (Kennett & Fine, 2008).

Overall, with these people lacking their so-called gut feelings and patients are able "to know but not to feel" This rather uniquely supports the model for morality is not about reasoning but emotional reactions instead.

To wrap up support for the model, Wheatley and Haidt (2005) got participants to be hypnotized and they were told to feel "a brief pang of disgust . . . a sickening feeling in your stomach" when reading an otherwise innocuous word, with the words being 'take' or 'often.'

Afterwards, the participants read several vignettes describing moral transgressions, half of which contained the hypnotic trigger word.

The results showed the participants rated the behaviours described in vignettes that included the trigger word as more immoral than the exact same behaviours described in vignettes that did not include the trigger word.

On the whole, in a strange way, this study does support the model because it shows people did not think or reason about the behaviour for it to be immoral. It was all about the emotion they felt when they read about the behaviour that made it immoral.

Personally, I really like looking at this model because I love seeing the creativity psychologists use to create experiments!

Schnall et al. (2008)

I certainly think this has to be one of the most creative studies I've read about because this study again focused on emotion and intuition as the cause of morality by recruiting 127 Stanford students from an outdoor space as the students walked past.

Then this is where the study gets creative because the participants were asked to answer a few questions and were randomly assigned into three conditions. The first was a control group, the second was called a mild stink condition where the participants were exposed to four sprays of fart gas into a rubbish bin near to them. The last condition was the strong stink condition where the participants had 8 sprays of fart gas.

Subsequently, the participants were required to

answer four questions about moral judgement involving these situations:

- legalization of marriage between first cousins
- approval of sex between first cousins
- moral judgments of driving rather than walking to work
- approval of a studio's decision to release a morally controversial film

The results found that the participants exposed to the fart spray, the dose didn't matter, were more severe in their moral judgments than participants in the control group.

The researchers decided to replicate the study in three more studies that tested morality in different measures of situational disgust.

Their results showed the participants with a greater levels of moral condemnation were the participants who completed the experiments in a filthy work area, study 2, had written about a time they had encountered something physically disgusting, Study 3, as well as the participants who had just watched a disgusting film clip in study 4 of the infamous toilet scene from the film *Trainspotting*. (And no, I haven't seen this film).

Overall, all these situations created strong negative emotional reactions for the participants and they all rated the various moral transgressions as more wrong than control participants. Showing the power and influence emotion has in morality.

Principle 2:

Moving onto the second principle, motivated social cognition is linked to morality because moral judgements and a person's morality serves a very important social purpose, and, like other forms of social cognition, morality can be biased.

Furthermore, research on motivated social cognition has shown that moral reasoning isn't like that of an idealized scientist or a judge seeking the truth. Instead, the research shows moral reasoning is like that of a lawyer or politician seeking whatever is useful to them. Regardless of whether it's true or not.

In other words, morality is made up of social cognition because morality is important to society and our social groups for reasons explained earlier in the chapter. But morality isn't perfect since it can be biased for our own personal gains.

Principle 3:

Continuing on with the principles of morality, we'll now be looking at how morality binds and builds us as humans.

Personally, at first I thought this was a strange idea but after I wrote this section I understood it a lot more and this is maybe the most interesting of the principles.

So, we know people do cooperate with strangers they'll never meet again and we make sacrifices for our social groups made up of people who aren't related to us. Hence, this shows morality builds and binds because it gets strangers to cooperate and work together.

Also, people attain their extreme group solidarity by forming moral communities and it's within these communities where selfishness is punished and virtue or moral behaviour is rewarded.

The principle is also shown in religious behaviour because whatever the origins of a person's religiosity, nearly all religions have culturally evolved a set of complex practices, stories, and norms that work together to suppress a person's self-concept and connect people to something beyond the self. Meaning, a religion's morality or moral code binds people together to practice the culture as a part of the religion.

Moreover, studies on rituals, particularly those involving some sort of synchronized movements that are common in religious rituals, like a ceremony, indicate that such rituals serve to bind participants together in what is often reported to be an ecstatic state of union.

Another way of viewing this principle is that people care a lot about morality and we all want to be seen as moral. Especially in the eyes of our ingroup members (van Nunspeet, Ellemers, Derks, & Nieuwenhuis, 2014). As well as research shows that moral judgments are biased by various factors, including our emotions (Schnall, 2017) and our attitudes (Bocian, Baryła, Kulesza, Schnall, & Wojciszke, 2018).

Interestingly, we can actually link this principle to politics because people selectively endorse some moral principles that allow them to rationalise moral conclusions that would be in line with their political orientation (Uhlmann, Pizarro, Tannenbaum, & Ditto, 2009). And we are more likely to perceive politicians as moral if their arguments and manifestos serve our interest and usurpingly deem other politicians that undermine our own interests as immoral. (Cislak & Wojciszke, 2006)

In addition, if we think about the principle in terms of social group and Social Identity Theory, people tend to view their own group as more moral than other groups. (Brewer & Campbell, 1976; Leach, Ellemers, & Barreto, 2007).

In my opinion, I always think it's interesting to try and look at things through different perspectives and just to find support from different theories. This is known as Theory Triangulation which I always think is a great idea in psychology research. As this prevents us from missing or overlooking any possible influence or factor that could affect what we're researching.

Overall, throughout this chapter, we've looked at morality because it does truly bind and build our social groups and morality is such a critical influence in our society. And we have one final chapter introducing us to the massive topic of morality and then we can start to see the different psychological factors influencing morality and later on, we'll look at moral grey areas.

We've got some great topics coming up.

INTRODUCTION TO BEING VIRTUOUS AND AMORAL

To wrap up this first section of the book so we can start looking at the different social, biological and psychological factors that impact our moral and immoral behaviour, there's one final area we need to be introduced to.

We need to understand virtuous and what being amoral is and you'll be introduced to some of the factors and research findings behind these examples of morality.

Therefore, we know that what we consider moral and immoral varies from person to person and in later chapters, we'll explore why this happens. Yet for now, we need to understand that there are variations and similarities in moral convictions and standards from culture to culture and religion to religion.

All these similarities stem from basic human

emotions.

Being Virtuous

When it comes to being a virtuous person, this is typically a person that holds themselves to a high ethical standard that has strong morals and acts in a moral way towards others. Whereas immoral people are thought of as evil, wicked and just not good people in the slightest.

Therefore, as this is the last introductory chapter, we're going to explore some basic questions that all of us have thought about at one time or another.

Are People Born With Morals?

Whilst there's an entire chapter dedicated to this topic later on, I want to mention that we used to think that babies were blank slates but research does show babies have an innate sense of morality. Then this is nurtured or discouraged by society and other social influences like parents.

Are Animals Moral?

I know there are certain people in the world that will hate what I am about to say, but humans are animals and animals are like humans. As a result, research shows that over 90% of animals do show some form of positive or even prosocial behaviour.

In addition, unlike humans, you never see mass warfare in animals and considering this is an immoral behaviour. Just like genocide, homophobia and racism, which you do not see in other animals despite homosexuality being present in over 1,500 species.

You could argue that animals are more moral than humans.

Can You Be Moral Without Being Religious?

I can definitely see me getting some hate emails because of this question and the question above. Since as you can expect, you don't need God or religion in the slightest to be a moral person because people are not fundamentally good or evil.

Although, in an effort to be balance I will mention that a Pew Study found that atheists are less likely to believe there are absolute standards of right or wrong.

Then again, not believing in a God or being religious doesn't undermine anyone's morality, but religious and non-religious people might have different ideas about morality.

Personally, I can understand this because I believe a woman having the right to choose what happens to their body is a moral behaviour. As is gender equality, homosexuality and all forms of equality. I strongly believe they are moral behaviours. But I know tons of religious people who I have had many conversations with think I am completely wrong and I am an immoral abomination.

In other words, no, you do not need religious to be a moral person.

What About Amorality?

After looking at virtuous behaviours and finishing off our introduction to moral behaviours, let's look at amorality. This is actually rather different from immorality because amoral people have no care or good sense of right or wrong. As well as amoral behaviours and this has always been of interest to people throughout the ages.

Mainly because we want to understand why do people do bad things.

One of the earliest examples of someone in power looking at amorality, or a good example I want to showcase here, is Pope Gregory the First in the 6th Century. Since he created the 7 deadly sins in Christianity with these sins being:

- Greed
- Anger
- Laziness
- Jealously
- Vanity
- Lust
- Gluttony

Generally, people who possess these deadly sins are seen in society as flawed and have no understanding of right or wrong.

As a result, let's look at some basic questions to help us have a deeper understanding of amoral behaviours.

<ins>What Is Amorality?</ins>

As I mentioned earlier if someone is amoral then they don't care about the difference between right and wrong, so they don't care about immorality or morality. Also, being an amoral person isn't about having a lack of understanding, amoral people actually do understand the difference between right and wrong.

Yet they do the immoral thing regardless.

One example of an amoral person is an amoral politician will have no conscience and they will instead make their choices based on their own personal needs. They won't even care if their choices and actions are right or wrong for their voters.

Can People Tell The Difference Between Right And Wrong?

Overall, yes, people do understand and they can tell the difference between what is right and what is wrong. Yet we have to understand ourselves, that what is right for one person is immoral for another person.

For example, I consider a woman right to choose what happens to her body to be a moral belief. Yet some people think a woman has no right to her own body. So I am immoral to some people.

At the end of the day, we need to remember that everyone's morality will be different because morality is based on a person's values, world experiences and upbringing. This means the moral divide between different cultures, even within a strong culture, can be massive.

Thankfully, all these factors and more will be explained in the next few sections of the book.

MORAL PSYCHOLOGY

PART TWO: INFLUENCES ON MORALITY

MORAL PSYCHOLOGY

ARE INFANTS MORAL?

As we continue with our look at what impacts our morality, I wanted to take a chapter to answer the somewhat "age old" question about whether infants are naturally moral or whether this is something they learn through social interaction, socialisation and through their culture.

Personally, I always hate these debates because they are unnecessarily reductionist by trying to reduce an immensely complex behaviour like morality down to a single cause. The debate says you are either born with morality or you learn it through your parents.

There is no in-between.

And that is why our next chapter is so interesting because you get to learn about the moral traits of infants and what the truth is behind this debate.

If you've ever wanted to know about infants and how moral they are, you'll enjoy this chapter for sure.

***

If you've been listening to The Psychology World Podcast for a while then you might have noticed that from time to time I report on research concerning the morality of infants. I've always found it is interesting and I like how research is starting to recognise that infants can be naturally moral. And yet this challenges a lot of traditional theories that have a lot of research support. Resulting in a rather large paradox for researchers. In this developmental psychology episode, you'll learn are infants moral by learning about a range of social and developmental factors that help to make infants moral (and immoral too). If you like learning about morality, prosocial behaviour and child psychology then you'll enjoy today's episode.

Are Infants Moral?

When it comes to the topic of morality in children and more specifically infants, there are generally two schools of thought. Firstly, you have the more traditional school of thought that has a lot of research support and this is the idea that children learn their morality through their parents. There are a lot of references in the Reference section at the bottom of the podcast episode, but one piece of evidence for this theory is how morality varies from culture to culture. This supports the social explanation of morality, because if morality was innate then morality wouldn't vary as much from culture to culture because our sense of morality would have evolved as part of our species.

Then another school of thought that has a

growing body of evidence comes from researchers like Yale Professor Karen Wyn. These researchers propose morality begins in infancy and this runs against the idea that morality is taught through parents.

How can there be so much evidence for both theories?

Could it be because they are both right?

There are a few different reasons about why Wyn and her critics are both right about morality and how it develops. Firstly, they're both right because the definition of morality varies slightly from study to study as does the level or measures of behaviour each study looks at. Since Wyn's research refers to an infant's innate propensity to be prosocial, whilst her critics focus on social conventions that differ from place to place.

I know this little example is silly in the grand scheme of things, but it is very apt here. In the UK, it isn't considered moral or immoral to put salt and pepper on your food, but in Portugal, it is considered rude and by extension, immoral to put extra salt and pepper on your world. Since you are implying the chef hasn't seasoned their food right.

As a result, it is possible that morality is an innate human trait that is universal in the human species but it is implemented and expressed differently between cultures and even from person to person. We only need to think about the different behaviours people think are moral within a single country or town, let alone an entire species.

What Did Wyn's Research Show?

In addition, Wyn found through her series of experiments that infants look longer at helping puppets than puppets that stopped another puppet from opening a box. As well as different variations of the experiment found the exact same thing, so this suggests infants prefer people who help others compared to people who made things more difficult for other people.

Of course, this research is only suggestive at this point in time, but what makes it interesting is that Wyn's study is part of a growing body of research making the same point. Infants do offer help, they do comfort people in distress and they prefer people who do the same.

Personally, I think this is actually a rather lovely and even heartwarming finding. Especially, because people like me who focus so much on clinical psychology, we read and focus on mental health conditions, mental health difficulties and the "darker" side of human behaviour from time to time. Therefore, this study is a pleasant reminder about the lighter side of human behaviour and how great psychology research can be.

Can These Prosocial Tendencies Be Overwritten?

Unfortunately, as you can probably guess, the innate sense of morality in an infant doesn't stay with an infant unless a parent builds on these propensities. Yet this isn't always just down to the parent, because these prosocial propensities can be overridden by peers and the larger culture as a whole if they convey very different values.

What Did Wyn Find Out About Prejudice?

An interesting finding of Wyn's study is that she found another trait that impacted the infant's judgements and this certainly isn't positive if you really think about it. So Wyn found that infants preferred the puppets who liked the same food as the infant. On the surface, this is a very normal finding that I wouldn't have cared less about, but Wyn makes a very interesting point that I can definitely understand.

She implied that this could be the root adult of prejudice because infants show we might prefer people who are like us and dislike people who are not like us. Remember, the babies also liked the puppets that were like them in terms of they shared similar interests in food, and at first, I thought this sounded like a silly example. But how many conversations as adults have all of us started and bonded over because of food?

A lot, so I think this food preference does hold ecological validity because it continues into adulthood. It was only a few days ago that me and a friend were having a conversation about nachos, and neither one of us are children.

Wyn talks about this finding more with the following quote:

"Babies and infants were far more likely to

approve of the similar puppets being helped, while having the same positive reaction when the puppets that chose different foods were hindered," Wynn said. "This reaction seems to suggest the roots of the adult impulses toward xenophobia, prejudice and war."

I think this is a very interesting point that will hopefully be researched more in the future.

Conclusion

Overall, at the end of this podcast episode, we know that infants have an innate sense of morality and what is morally right and wrong. Yet infants have a sense of "us and them" as well and this is important to realise when it comes to morality, because morality does account for in-group cohesion and this is something I'll talk more about in the future. And yet, morality and "us and them" thinking accounts for the violence that is found in religion as well according to the Philosopher John Teehan.

Therefore, I think the biggest takeaway from today's episode is to foster that sense of love, compassion and morality in our infants. We need to raise them to be moral, be kind and to be compassionate to other people, because that will help to make the world a better and safer place for everyone.

And isn't that the world we want to live in?

HOW DOES CATEGORISING OUR RELATIONSHIPS IMPACT OUR MORAL JUDGEMENTS?

As we continue our look at the social psychological factors that can impact our moral judgements, we need to turn our attention towards a facet I never really considered before now. The different types of social relationships we have in our lives.

Now as you'll see briefly in the psychology article below, I was rather surprised by this but when you really start to think about the types of behaviours we are willing to perform for our close friends compared to work colleagues this starts to make a lot of sense.

Please keep reading to find out how our social relationships impact our moral judgements.

***

Recently, I've been focusing a lot more on the psychology behind morality and what makes humans do "right" and "wrong" behaviours. A part of our morality is how we divide people up into different categories based on our relationship to them. This is a fascinating area of social psychology that I highly recommend you listen to today because you'll definitely learn a lot and you'll be thinking for sure. Therefore, in this social psychology podcast episode, you'll see the four types of different relationships people have, what these relationships involve and most importantly, how do these relationships impact moral dilemmas. If you enjoy learning about social relationships, decision-making and morality then you'll love today's episode.

<u>How Could Relationships Impact Morality?</u>

Now, I'll fully admit when I came across this research I wasn't entirely convinced that different types of relationships might impact different moral behaviours. Then I started thinking about it and I realised just how common this is. For example, two easy examples are, when I go out with a university friend of mine for dinner and it's the two of us, we both pay for our own dinners. That's what happens whenever I go out with friends to be honest. Yet I am willing to pay for the dinner of my closest friends because I'm closer to them and they're great. Whereas, if I'm having lunch with my friend that is also my supervisor (or will be in the future) at my

University's Parkinson's centre, I have absolutely no ethical problems with letting him pay for my lunch. He has the job and I help him out a lot so it is sort of only fair.

In that example, you can see three different examples of relationships and how I approach the very common idea of paying for a meal differently.

Are these really moral behaviours?

If you had asked me before this podcast episode, I would have said these basic examples have nothing to do with morality, but some researchers disagree. Especially because morality is all about what behaviours are right and wrong in a given situation. I'm sure some of you would say I shouldn't want my supervisor to always pay (granted we don't go out for lunch that often and I do not abuse that kind offer), but some of you would agree.

Then when we start thinking about additional factors, this gets more complex. For example, what if my friend is poor and struggles with money? Should I automatically pay for their dinners to help them out? Or what if I was struggling with money for a time? Is it morally right for me to ask my friend to pay me dinner so I could eat that night?

Some of you would say yes, others would say that was an immoral favour to ask.

That's why this is a great topic to look at.

What Are The Four Types of Relationships And How Do These Impact Morality?

Looking at the work of anthropologist Alan Fiske (1991), he categorises human relationships into four different types.

Firstly, you have communal sharing relationships where our ingroups are basically the same as us in relevant ways. Some examples of this would include teams at work, military units as well as our family.

Secondly, you have equality matching. These are relationships where we view others as our equals. Like, people who we take turns with at home or work, or people we take care to maintain our impartiality with. I know this one is a little complicated, but don't worry, I'll explain these categories in more detail in a moment.

Thirdly, you have authority ranking where we rank ourselves and others in a hierarchy or to a position. For instance, caste, work titles or seniority.

Finally, you have market pricing where we view others as a trade partner. These are people we view through a contractual lens. For example, people who we interact with because they help us because we help them and vice versa.

As a result of these categories, Rai and Fiske (2011) argue humans are motivated to behave differently toward each of these categories. And one example of this is we're happy to share resources with our family members but we get annoyed when a friend keeps asking us for stuff without a thank you, them spending time to cultivate our friendship and without reciprocating the favour.

Now, let's explore these in more depth.

<u>Communal Sharing and Morality</u>

When it comes to communal sharing relationships, these focus on an attitude of unity towards the ingroup. Since as we all know, maintaining any ingroup is not easy at times and there will be problems. Therefore, there is high motivation to maintain the ingroup because the people in the ingroup want to benefit the group over and beyond people outside the ingroup.

Due to ingroup members believe they have a common fate, which they want to be positive. Therefore, maintaining communal relationships relies on tribalism and in a sense keeping the tribe "pure". Resulting in ingroup members being morally motivated to eliminate these threats, even if they come at a very high moral price.

Interestingly, an international example of this communal sharing that Rai and Fiske (2011) mention is the Hutu Ten Commandments that mention how the unity as well as the fate of the Hutu people are perceived to be threatened by the Tutsi. Resulting in this fuelling propaganda that led to the Rwandan genocide.

A more personal example would be family attitudes towards kicking out LGBT+ members of the family. I know from personal experience and stories with friends how family units want to remain united and pure so there is minimal conflict that leads to family breakdown. So sometimes the easiest option is just to kick out the queer member of the family, making them homeless and completely cut off from the family.

Notice how I never said the easy option is the moral option?

It's disgusting but some families are just immoral.

Equality Matching and Morality

Our next type of relationship is focused on striking equal balances, which leads to a lot of positive ideas about morality. For example, human rights are thankfully all about treating other people as equals, governments should always treat people with dignity and respect, as well as we should treat others how we want to be treated.

In addition, striking an equal balance helps humans to cooperate in situations where we can't distribute resources equally or when it comes to taking turns.

Originally, we evolved these rules to limit free-riders because no one likes them at all. So this led to humanity developing some very elegant cooperation norms, like tit-for-tat so we can all generally trust each other in our economic and social interactions.

These norms generally work because people are motivated to maintain these rules and equality, because acting immorally or against these rules, results in punishment.

I always like reading anthropology research from

time to time because you get to learn about random tribes. Hence, the Hammurabi's code reflects the extreme lengths people can go to protect this balance, as does the ancient Babylonia ideal of an eye for an eye. Even today, there are many countries that continue to institutionalise balance-keeping by the process of capital punishment. A life for a life.

We could have an entire moral debate about the concept of "a life for a life" but I've already had that debate with some 15-year-old children this week, so I'm good and we generally understand how capital punishment and balance-keeping informs morality.

Authority Ranking And Moral Judgements

Whereas in these social relationships, people are motivated to maintain a hierarchy regardless of its type. This involves people respecting and deferring to an authority figure and this authority figure should provide protection and take responsibility to some extent for the subordinates' actions.

The easiest example of this is the military as well as military command structure and units.

Normally, this hierarchy and social relationship is beneficial for everyone involved. Since if we take a parental example, then a parent can demand respect from their young and vulnerable children. In exchange, the parent not only protects their children from harm but the parent comes to the child's defence too.

As you can see, it's useful for encouraging moral behaviour.

Unfortunately, this social relationship can cause immoral behaviour as well. For instance, people in leadership positions are often thought to be more entitled to the group's resources than other people. Like, CEOs having bigger offices, extra benefits and larger paychecks. I won't even get into that argument about whether this is moral or not. I think it depends.

Anyway, leaders can become corrupt and authoritarian too. Then if we remember Milgram's experiments, we realise subordinates are willing to follow extreme orders from authority figures even if it harms other people.

That is definitely not moral behaviour.

Market Pricing Impacting Moral Judgements

Our final type of social relationship comes from Market Pricing and these relationships are maintained by an in-between system of value to compare different goods. I get that was a weird explanation but what it means is this relationship is essentially an economic market where the people in these relationships are motivated to maintain proportionality.

In other words, make sure each other is providing equal value.

These economic principles can extend to the social world too, because when good and evil behaviours are weighed against each other, this is what people use to determine the best course of action.

If we look at the criminal justice system, juries

have to decide how much time a criminal should spend in prison in relation to the seriousness of the crime, we expect a system of meritocracy at work where the promotion or pay rise goes to the most deserving employee, and commanders are meant to determine how many lost lives are worth an action for the greater good.

How Do These Categories Mix and Conclusion

It's hard to think of any social relationships that are only one of these four types of relationships because there is a lot of overlap. For instance, if we think about dividing up a bill after a nice dinner, this is hard because going out with friends could be Equality Matching (because we want equal friendships) and it could be Communal Sharing to be honest. Or if you're out for dinner with a supervisor/ friend, it could be Authority Ranking, Equality Matching and Marketing Pricing.

On the whole, the entire point of today's episode is to show you that moral outrage as well as feelings get hurt because of these different types of relationships. Especially when they don't match your expectations.

For example, I know a lot of great trans people and a part of medical transitioning are different surgeries if they want them. Therefore, if a friend of mine had a surgery with a six-week recovery time and I helped them out for the majority of that time. And I would feel really good because I helped out my friend and I did the right moral thing in this situation. Then

I would be working on the assumption, this was a communal Sharing relationship because they're part of my ingroup and the common fate of the friendship group is tied together.

Then let's say if I later received an email and a bank transfer from my friend repaying me for my time and the email contained a list of the amount they were paying me for each thing I did for them.

This would be deeply hurtful because this friend would be categorising our friendship as a Market Pricing relationship instead of what I believed it to be.

Of course, this example has and will never happen, but similar hurt feelings have happened before to me. And this example is a good one showing how we categorise relationships impact our moral judgements. Because I'll tell you now I would never go above and beyond for a Market Pricing relationship in comparison to Communal Sharing relationship.

And this is a great little thinking exercise because we all have examples of these four relationships in our lives, so ask yourself this simple question:

How far would your moral behaviour go for the people in each type of relationship? Because there's a big difference between paying for a cheap dinner and being close enough to someone to want to spend six weeks with them after an operation.

What do you think?

HOW DOES SOCIAL INFLUENCE IMPACT MORALITY?

As part of the research process of this book, I had to look at a lot of my various psychology books to see when I had mentioned morality, and it turns out I've covered morality a lot more than I had originally thought.

Therefore, as we start to look at what social psychological processes impact morality and people's moral judgements, there was one area that shouted out to me.

Social influence.

Personally, I flat out love social influence because you have Milgram, Asch and so many other… interesting experiments. Yet I want to stress here that this does connect to morality in a number of ways.

Personally, we need to remember that social psychology as a subfield of psychology started as a result of World War Two with psychologists being interested in why the hell the Nazis did what they did. In other words, why did the Nazis commit such atrocities against innocent people?

This connects to morality because social influence made it possible and made the soldiers and other people involved in the Nazi's actions to think it was okay to commit their foul actions.

In addition, as you'll see throughout the next few chapters, conformity, obedience and other examples of social influence can all help to make someone do an action that they know is morally wrong.

The next few chapters have been adapted from Social Psychology, but they are powerful reminders of how social processes impact morality, and help to answer the question, why do people do bad things?

Social Influence

We are all influenced by others and social influence is the effect that other people can have on our thoughts, feelings and behaviour. As well as social influence can be divided into a few types including conformity, obedience as well as compliance and acceptance.

In addition, conformity can be good, bad or inconsequential. An example of good conformity is not pushing in a queue at a supermarket. Whereas compliance can change behaviour but not belief as well as acceptance is when you change your behaviour and belief.

For example, I comply with the social norm of

going to lectures at university but my belief is that sometimes just doing the reading and looking at the slides is more than enough.

Furthermore, Markus and Kitayara (1991) proposed that conformity is the 'social glue' that holds a society together.

Additionally, radicalisation is a special type of social influence where people are encouraged to strike out at a society that is deemed to be fundamentally wrong. (Ryan, 2007)

<u>Key Studies:</u>

Before we dive into the psychology and the theory of social influence and how it affects our behaviour. We need to learn several vital studies.

<u>Sheriff (1935, 1937)</u>

Sheriff was interested in the emergence of social norms.

Therefore, in his experiment he got participants to sit in a dark room and they had to observe a light. This led to the autokinetic effect- where you look at the light for a long time and you think it moves when it doesn't; then the light suddenly disappears.

Afterwards, the participant on their own is asked to estimate how much the light moved. Later, they do it again but are given two estimates from other participants.

The results show that when other answers were given, they convergent over time. Equalling a new social judgement norm. This norm persists over time when asked to rate it again, you continue the norm.

The reasons for these findings is the ambiguous stimulus; the light; gave the participants an internal frame of reference. This was combined with the differential judgement of others to create another frame of reference. Overall, with both frames of reference in mind, it was easier to give a value of movement. This created a norm in the process.

For example, if I thought 4cm but someone else said 6cm then I would have probably said 5cm of movement. Subsequently, over time as more and more answers got said a norm would develop as the difference between 5cm and 6cm is nothing in terms of social norms.

Morality Implications

Whilst I admit at first this study might seem like it has nothing to do with morality, I want to add that this study was about the development of social norms. Which is something that is a fundamental part of the development of morality and deeming what is right and wrong within society.

For example, if we think about one of the first chapters of the book and when Haidt had participants read the story about the brother and sister having sex. The reason why participants probably showed disgust was because this went against their internal frame of reference of "incest is just wrong because it is".

It's an idea at the very least.

Asch (1951, 1952, 1956)

In this study, the participant was seated 6th in a row of 7 people and they were presented with a diagram with a standard line to compare to 3 comparison lines. The participant needed to choose which comparison line matches the standard.

The experiment had three trials so in trial 1 everyone before the participant agreed on the same line. This was the correct one. For trial 2, everyone agreed on the correct line, but on trial 3 all confederates chose the wrong line.

Overall, the results showed that the control group; where everyone gave their answers individually; 99% of them chose the correct line. Compared to only 63% of the experimental group.

This is a brilliant quote from Asch (1955) because he summarises the results perfectly as the young people knew that the line was wrong but they chose it anyway.

'well-meaning young people are willing to call white black' (Asch, 1955)

Although, these findings are very interesting because in this situation there is no obvious pressure to comply, so it's odd that people do comply.

Morality Implications

Personally, I rather like Asch's study because it has no ecological validity, probably not a lot of temporal validity and the methodology... well, there are probably better ways to test this idea in our modern times.

Yet the point is still a good one.

The study clearly shows, and we all know this from our personal lives (not one of the few times social psychology is certainly common sense), when the majority of a social group deem something is right, other people will follow along.

Therefore, to use a moral example, if a lot of people deem killing a killer is morally right. Then there is an increased chance, someone else will agree to avoid breaking the consensus.

Overall, this small example of social influence could help us to understand why some people commit moral or immoral acts in certain situations. As well as this is an idea we'll continue to explore later on.

Milgram (1965, 1975)

Milgram's study must be one of the most famous psychology case studies because of how impressive and unethical it is.

This study wanted to examine the effects of punishment on learning, at least this is what the participants were told. In reality, the study was examining the effects of conformity.

Therefore, in the study, the participant was to teach another person a series of paired words and then test their memory, and if the participant got the words wrong then they would be punished with an electrical shock. The learner is a confederate trained on how to respond and the response that the participant heard were all recordings.

Additionally, the shocks ranged from a slight shock of 15 volts to 450-volts labelled XXX and the teacher was asked to deliver a higher level of shock each time the learner makes a mistake.

The Study's Procedure:

Firstly, the teacher; the participant; takes a mild electrical shock to know what it's like then they see the learner being strapped to a chair and electrodes attached to their wrists.

Subsequently, the teacher would continue to shock the confederate each time they got an answer wrong, as well as each time the participant wanted to stop shocking the confederate. They would be urged on by the researcher.

Interestingly, before the experiment began 110 experts said what they expected to happen in the experiment. These experts predicted that only 10% of people would exceed 110 volts and nobody would reach the 450 volts.

However, in reality, over 50% of people reach the 450-volt mark, but obedience decreased as shocks increased, as well as 63% of teachers went up and beyond the 450-volts.

Milgram's Other Studies:

Milgram conducted another 18 experiments with very similar results across all studies. He found that there was no difference in conformity for men and women as well as there were only a few cross-cultural differences.

These studies tell us that attitudes fail to determine

behaviour when external influences override them.

<u>Morality Implications</u>

Well, I think the moral implications are fairly clear because if an authority figure tells you to do something, you will probably do it.

<u>The Stanford Prison Experiment:</u>

This is another famous psychology experiment that is… beyond unethical.

The Stanford Prison Experiment happened in the summer of 1971; and whilst there are some modern questions about its findings; it stills shows the power of titles and social influence.

In the experiment, 24 participants were assigned to be prisoners or guards. The people who were prisoners were arrested, cuffed and taken to prison as well as they were processed like real prisoners.

In addition, the prison guards were dressed in a Khaki and wore sunglasses to dehumanise the guards.

On the first night, a prisoner rebellion sparked authoritative guard behaviour. Leading to the prisoners to be harassed and degraded.

In fact, this degradation got bad enough that the experiment had to stop after 6 days compared to the originally planned 14 days.

<u>Power of Situation:</u>

Both Milgram and the Stanford Prison Experiment argue about the power of the situation as some situations are evil. Leading to moral judgement to be suspended.

- 'The Lucifer Effect'- this is where a person crosses the line between good and bad and does an evil act.
- 'the banality of evil'. This is where a person doesn't believe they are committing evil instead they are doing a behaviour that society has normalised. (Hannah Arendt, 1963)

However, Adderly Eichmann was responsible for the Nazi 'final situation' and he willingly chose to do this act.

Therefore, it's not always about the situation as People often choose to be in a certain position (Blass, 1991).

Nonetheless, these studies were designed to allow evil to flourish and they were commanded by people in leadership roles who were given instructions to be 'evil'. Hence, it's possible that these studies lack ecological validity; where the experiment reflects the real world; as in the real world, nobody or only a few people are told to be evil. This questions the validity of the findings.

WHY PEOPLE CONFORM?

After looking at the possible effects and links between moral behaviour and social influence, it does raise questions about why on earth do people conform to the wants and decisions of social groups. For example, why the hell would someone conform to the order of an authority figure to shock someone until they were dead?

That's what we'll be looking at in this chapter.

Individual/Task Factor:

People are more likely to conform when the task they're doing is difficult so they conform as a way to get help, as well as people, conform when they feel uncomfortable and insecure.

Group:

Groups are extremely powerful things and they can make us do even more powerful things. Hence, why there's a whole chapter dedicated to groups- but these are the group factors that can cause conformity.

Asch (1955) found that groups of 3-5 people elicit greater conformity than groups of 1-2, yet after 5 people it makes no difference. This demonstrates how the group size can increase conformity rates.

Unanimity- Asch (1955) found if someone dissents then conformity only happens about 25% of the time. Hence, demonstrating how conformity can decrease as a result of deviants or people who don't conform.

Lastly, Milgram (1974) found that 'blue-collar' workers were most influenced by the 'professor'. Hence, showing the power of status in terms of conformity.

Contextual Factors:

As demonstrated in one of Milgram's studies they found that the further the authority figure was from the participant. The more obedience dropped.

This can be in terms of physical proximity like distance in metres or emotional proximity. Such as: being able to hear or see them.

This immediacy effect could possibly have something to do with us being closer to the learner. Allowing us to become more aware of their humanity and we are more likely to empathise with them.

Linking to the concept of dehumanisation; were seeing groups as less than human; allows people to justify atrocities against them. As shown in the Stanford Prison Experiment.

The legitimacy of the authority figure is important as well as people are sensitive to the legitimacy of the figure and they use this to determine if conformity is right or not.

Group Related Factors:

As demonstrated in another version of Milgram's classic study. He found that peer pressure is an important predictor of compliance, because when two participants were in the room and they both refused to go past a certain voltage point. Compliance dropped to as low as 10% Whereas two obedient peers raised compliance with 92.5%.

Overall, people use peers to judge the legitimacy and appropriate course of action.

Generally, groups who are unanimous and closely bound together are difficult to resist.

One explanation for this is that if the member's dissent then they risk the group's disapproval and social disapproval is a very powerful thing.

However, if someone has already vocalised a response then the pressure of the group can rarely change their mind. (Deutsch and Gerard, 1955)

This phenomenon is more than stubbornness because if a person goes against or reverses a decision then this can cause them to lose face, so they will often stick to their decision even if they lose out.

The similarity attraction hypothesis is linked to social influence as when people are in a setting with like-minded others (Abrams, Wetherdell, Cockhrane et al, 1990) and when a person has friends in the group (Thibaut and Stockland, 1956) conformity increases.

People can conform for two reasons:
- Normative influence- the social influence that arises from the need to gain social approval from others.

Basically, 'you go along with the crowd' to meet people's positive expectations.

Interestingly with a normative influence attempt, people are more likely to disagree with the group, but they suppress their disagreement in order to be liked.
- Informational influence- the social influence that comes from the desire to be correct so they can accept information from others.

Particularly happens in an ambiguous social setting.

Referent Information Influence:

This is when we are socially influenced to conform to a group because we are members and adherence to group norms defines us as a member.

For example, as a member of my university's baking society, I always adhere to the norms of being social and having fun because in order to be a part of the group I need to follow these norms.

Who is influenced?

Many social psychologists argue that there are personality types or characteristics that make people more likely to be influenced.

However, there is no research to support these claims and there are a lot of contradictory or weak findings. (Mischel, 1969)

Equally, the research is very mixed and

inconclusive about gender differences towards conformity as some research suggests that women are susceptible to influence.

However, Milgram (1974) and Eagly (1987) and other studies haven't found such claims.

However, experimental design can be important as these tasks can be more familiar to men. Leading women to be less sure and a lower conformity rating.

<u>Minority Influence:</u>

After looking at the reasons why people conform and how people are affected by social influence. In this last section, we will be focusing on how minority groups can influence people. As a result, this is difficult to do and this is how most social movements start off, as a minority. The process of minority groups gaining influence is called innovation.

Interestingly, minority influence wasn't investigated until the 1960s after the women's rights movement but during the black right movements by Moscovici.

Consequently, Moscovici (1976) found that the influence of minorities can't be accounted for by the same principles that explain majority influence.

As a result, there are fewer people in these minority groups, they have less control and they have less access to information.

Therefore, he argued that the minority's impact lies in their own behavioural style because their behaviour needs to be clear, consistent over time (diachronic consistency) and stable over time.

Synchronic Consistency:

This type of consistency states that minority group members all need to be on the same page. Otherwise, they won't be as effective.

Moreover, minority groups are less likely to be influenced by normative influence because there is no normality pressure from the majority.

On the other hand, most influence occurs on a more private level and being in the minority groups evokes a validation process, so the person feels like their opinions are right.

Lastly, as the participant thinks more closely about issues. The participants become more likely to be privately influenced However, majority pressure may prevent this from being shown publicly.

CONTROVERSIES OF THE EXPERIMENTS

A few chapters ago, we spoke about a number of experiments that suggest the power of the situation. Personally, I love those studies because they're useful, interesting and they show why Ethical Guidelines are beyond critical. Despite their extremely unethical procedure.

However, in this chapter, I'm going to talk about some more questionable aspects of the research.

When I was taught this at university, I was very interested in this topic since no one talks about it.

<u>What Was Reported Vs What Happened:</u>

In all honesty, the quotes will show more than I will but Nicholson (2011) found some very interesting results.

Firstly, in Milgram (1964) "all participants were told that the victim has not received dangerous electric shocks"

In reality, after the experiment, they weren't told this straight away, as supported by participants who said: "I was pretty well shook up for a few days after the experiment. It would have helped if I had been told the facts shortly after"; "I seriously question the wisdom and ethics of not completely dehoaxing each subject immediately after the session" and "I actually checked the death notices in the New Haven Register for at least two weeks after the experiment…"

I think this is appalling because just imagine checking to see if you had killed anyone for two weeks after your experiment.

Intense Distress:

Another interesting point was Milgram (1965/1972) admitted they caused intense distress, but they insisted that post-experiment screening revealed no lasting harm.

Yet again, Nicholson (2011) found participants said differently.

For example:

- "I was…. just completely depressed for a while"
- "By coincidence, a fellow employee had taken part in the same experiment… Later we compared notes… during one of our discussions I… said things I normally never would say… I used some vulgar words and

shortly thereafter because of other conditions I lost my job"

- "Since taking part in the experiment I have suffered a mild heart attack…. I feel it is imperative you make certain that any prospective participant get a clean bill of health"

Again, I think this is disgusting that one experiment had such devastating consequences.

On the other hand, I am extremely glad we have the measures we have in now and the ethical guidelines.

Off-Script:

This point I found weird and comical since Griffs & Whitehead (2015) found the experimenters in the Milgram study went off-script.

Due to the four prompts were never meant to be coercive techniques. They were meant to be stopping points of the experiment.

Meaning the funny part of the experiment was the only reason why the study got the results it did was because of these coercive techniques.

Perry (2013b, p223) suggested that this new content began to sound much more likely bullying and coercion when you listen to the material.

Additional Research Problems:

Another problem with these studies as Carnahan & McFarland (2007) found fewer people would volunteer for a 'psychological study of prison life' compared to a 'psychological study'.

Therefore, you get a very bias sample since the people that signed up for the study were more aggressive, more narcissistic, authoritarian, machiavellian, (the willingness to manipulate others for personal gain) Social Dominance Oriented and less altruistic as well as empathic.

Overall, this makes for a very poor research sample because all these participants were not the average person.

Therefore, this only adds to the debate surrounding the generalisability of the findings.

<u>Lack of Ecological Validity:</u>

Whilst, we're all pointing out the problems with these major studies. We must add that the studies were carefully created to allow 'evil' to flourish and in the real world, it could be more difficult for evil to flourish. Due to several confounding variables.

Afterwards, the situations were maintained as well as worsened by individual behaviour. This can be clearly seen in the Stanford Prison Experiment where the guards did what they did because the researchers gave them no guidance.

As supported by these instructions by Zimbardo to the guards at the beginning of the experiment:

"We can create in the prisoners feelings of boredom, a sense of fear to some degree, we can create a notion of arbitrariness that their life is totally controlled by us, by the system, you, me… They'll have no freedom of action, they can do nothing, or say nothing that we don't permit. We're going to take away their individuality in various ways."

One important thing to note about these vague instructions is that these are as detailed as the instructions during the holocaust. This made the guards need to be more creative and devise torture methods.

This feeds into the idea that it is the situation and people that interact to create good and evil. (Haslam & Reicher, 2007, Review) Since the prison situation didn't make evil, and the guards alone weren't evil before they interacted with the situation.

Two major factors play additional roles in the creation of evil because identification plays an important role (Levine & Crowther, 2008; Reicher & Haslam, 2006) as does ideology. For example, ideologies about dominance and equality. (Sidanius et al., 2003).

As a result, people who highly identify with the role of guard and has high ideologies around dominating people. These people are likely to be more 'evil' when interacting with the situation.

<u>Does This Reduce Validity?</u>

Now that you know all the research problems with this study, we need to question *do these problems make the study any less valid?* Or another way of putting it is *does this study still measure what it intended to?*

This question is raised because real world perpetrators of atrocities are unlikely to be polite in their requests. Possibly giving the study its validity because the way the experimenters asked the participants their requests matched the real world.

Can This Be Ethically Replicated?

To truly find out if the Milgram studies do have validity, we need to replicate them, but can we do this considering their unethical nature?

Thankfully we can replicate them by reducing the distress the participants experienced, capping the shocks at 150 volts which doesn't matter because 80% of 'teachers' got all the way according to Burger (2009). Suggesting the Milgram studies still have validity.

Two other ways of replicating these studies include the clever use of virtual reality experiments. As done by Slater et al (2006, UCL Studies) as well as by using immersive digital realism as seen in Haslam, Reicher & Miller (2015)

Do the Basic Findings Still Replicate?

Even the replication studies and methods outlined above, are the findings from the Milgram studies still applicable?

The answer seems to be yes because Dolinski et al (2017) redid the experiment, with adaptations of course, with the top level being 450 volts and it was not XXX like in the Milgram studies. However, despite this change 90% of participants got to 450 volts just like in Milgram's studies.

Again, this is further supported by Beauivous et al (2012) who did this with TV producers so participants believed they were in a gameshow and had to shock people up to 450 volts. The results showed many, many people complied.

A final experiment from Damburn and Vatire (2012), where participants were made aware from the start, the learner was a confederate only acting, found 32% of people obeyed to 450 volts, and this increased to 50% of people when they could hear, not see the confederate.

On the whole, the answer is yes. The results might be shocking but they still replicate.

Was It Really Blind Obedience?

A major critic of the original Milgram study was that it wasn't counterbalanced nor did it have a control group. As well as the experimenter ensured that you would continue when he gave you the second prompt. This prompt could be powerful and signified them to be good participants.

Caspar et al (2016) did a replication of Milgram's basic setup with a coercive vs free choice condition and they examined whether people had the psychological experience of free choice. They found under the coercive condition, people felt less responsible for their actions. Also, they felt time go quicker. This study suggests the results were not down to blind obedience like the study suggested.

Are Groups Always More Risky?

I know the past few chapters have been depressing reads that show the downsides of human behaviour and social groups.

But I want to stress social groups aren't always riskier than being alone.

For example, Abrams, Hopthrow, Hulbert and Frings (2006) studied risk orientation in groups compared to people alone and after consuming alcohol vs a placebo.

Their results showed when people were alone, people found riskier choices more attractive. This was eliminated when in groups.

HOW DID MORALITY EVOLVE?

So far we've looked at a lot of social and environmental factors that influence our morality, but is it possible our biology can impact our morality?

It turns out the answer might be yes because there is a growing amount of research into the evolutionary and genetic basis of morality. Therefore, in the psychology article below, we'll understand how morality and cooperation behaviours evolved and we'll even touch on why we experience moral conflict.

***

Cooperation is found in all human cultures all over the world, because people help each other, support the ingroup and help others to be successful. This implies that cooperation behaviours evolved in the human species to help us survive and thrive, and people that didn't cooperate died off. This is important to consider because cooperation behaviour is the basis of morality and doing what is morally right and wrong. Therefore, in this biological psychology podcast episode, you'll learn how did cooperation behaviours evolve, how this helps us and how cooperation behaviours impact our morality. If you enjoy learning about behaviour, cooperation and evolutionary psychology then you'll enjoy this episode for sure.

How Did Cooperation Evolve?

Before we look at evolution specifically, I want to mention how we can study the advantages of different behavioural strategies to help us understand cooperation, and Game Theory provides us with a good theoretical framework to work with.

Therefore, game theory gives us a way to understand what actions are beneficial to our genetics and this tells us which ones are likely to have evolved over time. As well as this helps us to understand morality too because we can study moral strategies that are more likely to propagate genes. Allowing us to implicit what morals have likely evolved.

Then when this has been combined with the empirical studies we have on the presence of these specific moral values all over the world, we can start to understand at a deep level the sort of moral decision-making processes people like and support.

As a result, Oliver Scott Curry and his team wanted to understand the psychological mechanisms that play a role in our moral behaviour, so they took game theory and he made the case that there are at least seven types of moral principles that guide human cooperation to greater or lesser degrees around the world. This has been supported with growing amounts of evidence too.

What Are The 7 Moral Principles?

Loyalty And Family Treatment

According to Curry's research, the first moral principle is loyalty to the ingroup. Since non-zero-sum games, or as you and me will call them win-win or lose-lose situations, confer genetic survival advantages when people can coordinate themselves to pull off a task that they simply cannot do alone. For example, one person cannot starve off rivals for resources but a group of people could. This connects to morality because humans place loyalty as an important skill that (if I get poetic for a moment) the oil that helps to spin the wheels of coordination and cooperation within a person's own community. These tasks benefit the self and others in the ingroup too.

Secondly, another moral principle is preferential treatment of their own family. Since the more genetics you share with a person, the more likely you are to help the person. This is important from an evolutionary point of view because it's more strategic to help our siblings compared to our cousins or even strangers. Which is why our morals tend to compel us to be more altruistic towards our own flesh and blood. As well as this sense of duty to help and care for our loved ones is a common sight throughout the world.

Deference and Heroism

Thirdly, and this is an interesting one, a moral principle is deference. I think this is a weird one because I don't naturally associate deferring to authority as a moral behaviour, maybe I think it's a neutral behaviour. Yet the evolution of morals does involve people deferring to "superior" parties, because research has found that people value qualities such as obedience, respect and humility. As well as people who have these qualities are judged as moral but if people don't show respect and aren't humble (just two examples I know), these people are seen as immoral.

Just think about us judging a disrespectful child as immoral when they're shouting and not listening to a parent. That's a good, everyday example of difference.

On the other hand, heroism is a moral principle because when we live in social groups and we have to deal with scarce resources, at some point there will be conflict over resources. Therefore, this means not everyone can get what they want and it's important for everyone that the conflict is settled before it gets too costly.

As a result, one way to resolve the conflict is to understand who is likely to win in the first place and defer to that person.

This connects to moralism and cooperation in an interesting way because the values that signal to others they're capable of winning a conflict include skilfulness, heroism, confidence amongst a few others.

Therefore, if we connect deference and heroism together. Then we understand a person who defers to others is seen as moral if they're obedient, respectful and humble. As well as the "superior" party who is high in heroism is seen as moral as long as they have high confidence, high heroism, high skilfulness amongst a few others.

It's this section specifically that helps me to understand that morality truly, truly is all about perspective and how others see you.

Reciprocity

Another moral principle is reciprocity because we need to be able to give something away with the idea that we will receive something else in return. This is the basic premise of cooperation, because if we help our friends for example, then we expect our friends to be something nice for us in return. Also, I've mentioned this somewhere else in the book but our focus on "tit-for-tat" is a useful way of getting rid of free riders. Then if we connect this to evolution, it is a person's moral capacities for trust, anger, guilt, apologising, retribution and gratitude that helps to facilitate the social exchanges that cooperation relies on. Which in turn typically increases genetic fitness allowing it to be passed on to the next generation.

Possession And Dividing Up Equally

A final important aspect of cooperation is how to peacefully divide up resources to reduce conflict and act in a moral way by helping others in need. There are two moral principles that are important for this idea of peacefulness.

Firstly, possession is important because around the world, it is typical to find that people honour the notion that whoever owns or has prior possession of the resource gets continued access to it. For example, if I owned a potato farm then people would honour the fact that I possess the farm so I should get continued access to my own farm. Then I will act morally and distribute my crops to everyone else in turn.

Also, this suggests there is a global seen of property rights and people feel wronged when we have something that belongs to us stolen.

Secondly, the whole idea of peacefully dividing up resources relies on people dividing up the resources fairly, because we need to distribute the limited resources we have whilst decreasing conflict. Any resource-related conflict can be decreased by there being a shared agreement in place saying how these resources are going to be divided up. And people use two ways to divide limited resources. The first one is possession which we just focused on.

Then the other one comes from a sense of justice and fairness where everyone gets the same amount of resources, or people get the amount of resources equal to the amount of effort they exerted to get the resource. For instance, a good example of this would be getting paid per hour because someone who works

6 hours compared to 8 hours in a day hasn't exerted as much effort as the 8-hour person (in theory) so it is only morally right that the person who did the 8-hour shift got more of financial resources.

<u>Conclusion</u>

Looking at morality through game theory is useful for investigating the wide range of moral principles that guide our moral behaviour, and it explains why we can be morally conflicted as well.

Since sometimes we need to allocate extra time and attention to our struggling siblings, but this might increase our wants for reciprocity. Or maybe our superiors have taken way too much credit for our work and we know we should be humble and defer to them, but we aren't sure if we should be protective of our work and let us get the credit we deserve.

So what is the best course of action when different moral principles conflict with each other?

Well, that's the insanely fun thing about morality. There isn't a right or wrong answer at the end of the day, even if we look through a genetic and evolutionary perspective.

WHY IS MORALITY POWERFUL?

At the end of this second section, I wanted to step away from different factors that influence moral behaviour and instead I wanted to look at why is morality important in the first place.

How does morality benefit us? How could morality benefit our mental well-being? How could morality help to make the world a better place?

All those great questions will be answered in this chapter and I have to admit it was a very heartwarming and positive chapter to write, which just makes learning about it even more fun.

***

The vast majority of people believe that acting in a morally right or morally wrong way isn't that powerful, but research shows it can have a lot of mental health benefits. Especially, as morality is about acting and behaving according to a set of standards that are largely influenced by our life experiences, character and worldview. Some people have a more innate sense of morality and fairness, and some do not. But why does morality matter. In this social psychology podcast episode, you'll learn why morality is powerful and why morality is always important to think about. If you enjoy learning about moral behaviour, social psychology and mental health, then you'll love today's episode.

Why Is Morality Powerful?

For a change, what I wrote in the introduction to this psychology article isn't standalone. Since continuing with what I said earlier, moral behaviour is about behaving and acting according to a set of standards and whilst there are social norms for moral behaviour, there are a lot of variations with each person considering what is normal and what isn't.

Let's take the most interesting example about taking another life. The general moral guideline is a human shouldn't kill another person under any situation whatsoever. Yet there are some people that think killing criminals is perfectly okay, others do not. Some people believe killing in self-defence is okay, whilst others think this is outrageous. Also, some people think killing people breaking into your home is okay, but others do not.

That is just one small example of the huge variations there are in moral judgements that differ from person to person.

Therefore, the very idea of morality is somewhat flexible and it allows us to interact as a society, that is the main goal of morality. Since when we perform in a moral way, we're stepping away from our own self-interest and we're thinking and acting in a way that benefits our social groups and society as a whole.

Interestingly, there are authors and philosophers like Jonathan Sacks, who believe that being moral is about being "anti-self-help". In other words, he believes that acting in a moral way is about us being able to focus on strengthening our relationships with other people. This is a quote from his book *Morality: Restoring the Common Good in Divided Times*. Morality is about "responding to their needs, listening to them, not insisting that they listen to us, and about being open to others,"

And the reason why this quote is important is because when we listen to other people (whether these are typically people we listen to and agree with or not), we can be transformed by that experience.

Sacks believed that the strongest countries in the world should listen to and help the weak and the vulnerable. He believed this because "if we care for the future of democracy, then we must recover this sense of shared morality which binds us as a collective. There is no liberty without morality, no freedom without responsibility, no viable *I* without the sustaining *we,*"

Personally, it is that idea of "I" and "we" that I quickly want to talk about, because I cannot afford to say too much because this is not a political podcast. Yet social psychology is built about the idea of ingroups and outgroups because this is how the world works. And yet, Sacks is right about if we want to live freely, happily and have the ability to do whatever we want then we have to start thinking about working with groups we don't normally listen to. The polarisation of the Western world isn't about working and coming together and it isn't about a collective "we", it is about the "I" in a small, divided and deeply divided world. And Sacks is right, we can all divide ourselves and act in ways that only help "I"s and our individual small social groups, but that isn't sustainable in the long term.

If the collective "we" falls then the "I"s cannot exist and by the time we realise we face losing "I"s then it will already be too late to save the collective "we" whatever that means to you.

That is probably the most political thing I have ever said on this podcast but I hope I've kept it vague enough to not lose too many listeners.

Research Support On The Power of Morality

Tan (2020) conducted a study on mindfulness and this researcher is an educator by trade and in the paper, there is a lot of talk about Confucius. As well as whilst Confucius didn't know the term morality back then, this is basically what he was talking about with his concept of Jing.

In addition, Tan talked about morality, mindfulness and the COVID-19 pandemic. Especially, about how our heightened states of anxiety was caused by the increasing amounts of uncertainty that people experienced. Let alone because of the huge personal and economic damage the pandemic brought and the major disruptions it caused in our social and healthcare systems.

Furthermore, Tan pointed out how the pandemic brought out the collective consciousness of us because people took part in mask-wearing, handwashing and social distancing behaviours. Not only to protect themselves but the larger social group as a whole. Yet Tan pointed out how "the global crisis has brought out the worst in human beings such as selfishness that stems from panic" (page 6). For example, the overstocking of items that other people desperately need. And it is this overstocking that is inconsiderate, possibly immoral and it isn't mindful of the collective "we" that exists in each country and the larger world.

Finally, Waytz and Hofman (2019) found that thinking and acting morally can enhance our positive feelings about ourselves and it improves our psychological well-being. Therefore, there is a lot of talk about the importance of self-care but it is important to note how our moral actions might benefit other people too.

Conclusion

Overall, at the end of this podcast episode, we understand that morality can be a powerful force for good in the world, because morality can get us to listen, help and support others that we might not in normal situations. Since being moral is about helping the collective "we" instead of the "I" and it is that moral behaviour that can help improve our well-being and our self-esteem.

Therefore, in case you're wondering what are some basic moral behaviours that might help you, here are some of you to think and hopefully act on in the future. You can prevent and do no harm to others, you can have good intentions, know yourself by acknowledging your positive and negative behaviours, help people in need, smile, be emotionally supportive and offer other people praise.

I know those moral behaviours sound so simple, but they are so effective and so important. It is great to people others, it is great to be supportive and help those in need, and a lot of great feelings can come from just doing the right thing and helping someone. So maybe we should all challenge ourselves this week and try to do at least one moral behaviour each day this week.

And hopefully, we'll make another person's day better each day this week and helping to improve 7 people's days. Now wouldn't that be a brilliant thing to do.

PART THREE: GREY AREAS OF MORALITY

MORAL PSYCHOLOGY

INTRODUCTION TO MORAL GREY AREAS

Out of all the sections in the book, this one has to be my absolute favourite. All the other sections of the book are interesting, engaging and fascinating, but personally I loved researching this section. Since it helps us to answer a very basic but extremely complex question about human behaviour.

Why do people do questionable things?

We've already looked at the wide range of different situational, social and environmental factors in the last section that influence morality, but now we get to truly focus on grey areas. Areas were there isn't a clear definition of what is morally right and morally wrong.

As a result, because in terms of definitions and morality more generally, this can get a little complex. This section uses this chapter as an introduction where I will hammer home what morality is, before talking about moral grey areas. Then the rest of the chapters in this section will be dedicated to looking at psychological factors and mechanisms that allow moral grey areas to develop.

I am so excited about those chapters, they're great fun.

Reminder Of Morality

Morality is all about what is "good", "ethical" or "right" in a given situation as well as this is the way that people are meant to behave (Haidt, 2012; Haidt & Kesebir, 2010; Turiel, 2006). For example, we shouldn't kill, lie or hit people.

In addition, we have moral guidelines that help us to do what is morally right and prevents harm coming from immoral behaviours. Also, these moral guidelines can get us to carry out performances that have no or little direct benefit to us. For instance, if we really think about fairness, empathy and altruism are all next to useless for us from a self-centred viewpoint, because it doesn't help us get ahead. Whereas selfish behaviours would help us.

However, the moral rules and guidelines that society has created for itself, as well as the negative consequences for breaking these moral rules, help people to come together to live in social communities. And in our social communities, these moral rules help us to prevent selfish behaviours, lying behaviours and a whole host of other moral behaviours (Ellemers, 2017; Ellemers & Van den Bos, 2012; Ellemers &

Van der Toorn, 2015).

Because we don't want to get punished for these immoral behaviours.

<u>Role of Morality In Social Order</u>

Furthermore, morality is important for maintaining social order as well (this is something we look at in more depth in the next section of the book) and this is agreed by a wide range of academics from different fields.

For example, evolutionary scientists and biologists have demonstrated in their research that empathetic as well as selfless behaviour is important in communities of animals that live together. Also, when we consider that humans originated from communities of animals then we can consider these animal communities the origins of human morality too (de Waal, 1996).

As a result, this work mainly focuses on how groups show altruism, empathy and fairness in face-to-face groups, where everyone knows and depends on each other.

<u>What Is First Tier Morality?</u>

We can learn more about this in an analysis done by Tomasello and Vaish (2013) because they termed this as the "first tier" of morality. This is where people can observe and copy the treatment they receive from others to elicit and reward empathetic and cooperative behaviours that help to protect both the individual and group survival.

<u>What Is Second Tier Morality?</u>

In addition, a lot of political scientists, legal scholars and philosophers have helped to expand this idea, because they've addressed more abstract principles about morality that people use to govern and regulate an individual's behaviour in larger and more complex societies when compared to more primitive communities of animals (Haidt, 2012; Mill 1861/1962).

This is needed because as we can imagine, compared to the behaviour needed in communities of animals, the nature of empathetic and cooperative behaviours in large-scale human societies is more complex and symbolic. Due to most of the time, our interactions depend less on any sort of direct exchanges between two people, but instead morality taps into the abstract concept of the "greater good".

I seriously doubt a pride of lions or a herd of Zebras need to think about the "greater good".

Therefore, academics have focused on how specific behaviours might or might not be guided by different moral guidelines and principles that might institutionalize social order according to such principles (Churchland, 2011; Morris, 1997).

Now we'll link theory to practice a little bit more.

As a result, this is what Tomasello and Vaish (2013) consider the "second tier" of morality. This is where morality focuses on its social signalling functions and it is this tier that helps to distinguish human and animal morality (Ellemers, 2018).

Because animal morality focuses on survival, but

at this tier, human morality loses this immediate survival-focus to a large extent. Yet different specific behaviours can gain a more abstract survival value and be prescribed by society as morally "right" even though they are generally meaningless from a survival viewpoint.

For example, let's take specific dress codes, and let's use a hot topic at the time of writing. I have heard that some people (bigots) believe that transgender individuals should not be allowed to dress to reflect their gender identity, and some people (bigots) call this behaviour as immoral. This is an interesting one because whether someone sticks to a socially prescribed dress code or not has no immediate survival value, but people still prescribe a moral judgement to it.

Or maybe a clearer example is the idea of it being morally wrong for young women to dress inappropriately short dresses because that makes them immoral people. I hate to imagine how many times I've seen that judgement play out in the media, my social world and attitudes towards rape victims. Therefore, if we look at what I just said, making a moral judgement about the length of someone's skirt has no immediate survival value to the group or the individual, but society still prescribes a moral judgement to it.

Humans really are weird.

Consequently, specific behaviours can acquire this symbolic moral value to such an extent that they define how people mark their religious identity, communicate their respect for authority, or secure group belonging for those people that adhere to these moral judgements (Tomasello & Vaish, 2013).

On the whole, moral judgements can function to help maintain social order because certain moral judgements rely on complex explanations, so this requires verbal exchanges to communicate how these "moral" guidelines for these behaviours actually work.

This is no different than telling a small child not to shout and scream during a wedding, funeral or when someone else is talking. The parent needs to tell the child not to do that because the "no shouting or screaming" immoral behaviour is made-up by society and society has deemed it immoral (and I agree).

As you can tell, these specific moral behaviours require language-driven attribution and interpretation to capture this symbolic meaning that isn't always obvious on the face of the behaviour and visible indicators of emotions (Ellemers, 2018; Kagan, 2018).

In other words, going back to our parent and child example, the child needs the parent to tell them not to shout and scream during a wedding, because this isn't automatically clear to them. Since the meaning of this moral guideline is symbolic and abstract until they're told this is a guideline.

Rest Of The Section

Now that we understand morality at a deeper level and we understand the theory behind "second tier" morality, in the rest of the chapters in this section, we're going to explore different behavioural approaches that can help us to understand morality.

All three of these approaches can easily be characterised as "second tier" (Tomasello & Vaish, 2013) morality because they all go beyond the human behaviour aspects of empathy and altruism like what we see in communities of animals.

Personally, I think these 3 approaches are really fun and interesting so let's turn over the page and explore these mechanisms that explain how humans behave in moral grey areas.

MORAL PSYCHOLOGY

WHAT IS THE SOCIAL ANCHORING OF RIGHT AND WRONG?

Considering that moral grey areas focus on times when there are no clear right or wrong choices, we need to understand how we come to know what is deemed morally right or wrong in the first place. We largely learn this through how different actions are socially judged by other people.

In addition, researchers stress that what is morally right and wrong differs depending on the theoretical perspectives being taken. For instance, Skitka (2010) and their peers convincingly argued that beliefs about what is morally right or wrong aren't the same as other attitudes or strongly held beliefs that people have (Mullen & Skitka, 2006; Skitka, Bauman, & Sargis, 2005; Skitka & Mullen, 2002). Instead, strongly held moral beliefs are seen as strong mandates that compel someone to act in a certain way in a certain situation.

In terms of the social group, moral convictions or strongly held moral beliefs are useful guidelines that we expect others to follow. As well as this explains why we get emotionally distressed when other people don't follow our moral guidelines.

In other words, we get distressed when people act immorally towards us or others.

Yet the effects of people violating our moral convictions doesn't just stop at emotional distress, because we can find these people intolerable and some people might even commit violence against people who challenge their views (Skitka & Mullen, 2002).

Furthermore, the social definition of what is right and wrong has been focused on in a range of theoretical perspectives looking at moral behaviour. For instance, the Theory of Planned Behaviour (Ajzen, 1991) gives researchers a framework that clearly explains how our behavioural intentions are determined by our own personal dispositions and social norms held by self-relevant other people (Ajzen & Fishbein, 1974; Fishbein & Ajzen, 1974).

Therefore, this theory is useful when it comes to morality because research using this perspective has been used to show that the adoption of moral behaviours, like expressing care for the environment, can be enhanced when relevant others think this is important (Kaiser & Scheuthle, 2003).

Furthermore, this has been shown in other ways

too because Haidt (2001) argued that our judgments about what are moral or immoral behaviours or even character traits are specified in relation to *culturally defined virtues*.

And this is good to note because what different cultures think is morally good or bad does differ and this helps us to understand how morality can vary between different cultures. This doesn't just apply to social groups and how different social groups within a culture help to define morality, because how a culture defines morality can be influenced by political and religious factors too (Giner-Sorolla, 2012; Haidt & Graham, 2007; Haidt & Kesebir, 2010; Rai & Fiske, 2011).

In addition, Haidt (2001) goes on to explain and specify that our moral intuitions are developed by implicitly learning our peer group's norms and through cultural socialization. This argument has been supported by different empirical studies showing how moral behaviour plays out in groups (Graham, 2013; Graham & Haidt, 2010; Janoff-Bulman & Carnes, 2013).

Therefore, this body of research shows us the different factors that different social groups use in their moral reasoning (Haidt, 2012). Meaning if we connect these different judgments about what is moral and immoral to different people's social groups and social identities, this helps us to understand why different social, political and religious groups differ so much on what they consider to be moral and immoral behaviour. As well as this helps us to understand why different groups struggle to understand the point of view of other groups (Greene, 2013; Haidt & Graham, 2007).

Personally, I think a great way to understand this idea is by looking at a western country or western context the majority of us might be familiar with. If we look at the position of Catholics, a right-wing party and a left-wing party on abortion. We can generally understand that each of those three groups or to be honest, subcultures within a society have different positions on abortion.

As do their members.

Therefore, the right-wing and Catholics tend to be flat out against abortion but for different reasons. The right-wing party could consider abortion immoral because of the political context of the social group. Whereas the Catholics might consider abortion wrong in the religious context that their social group provides them. Then left-wing parties are generally okay with abortion because it is considered moral behaviour in that particular social group.

That's just a little example of how the political, social and religious contexts found within a social group can influence and anchor what is deemed moral and immoral behaviour.

Conclusion

On the whole, from this chapter we can learn that these research studies suggest that moral guidelines can be in based, at least in part, on the moral and immoral judgements that are essentially made up by a culture through social norms.

Due to its these ideas about moral and immoral behaviour that come from what people inside different social groups think are important and these people hope that other group members will stick to these moral behaviours that anchor the group together (Ellemers, 2017; Ellemers & Van den Bos, 2012; Ellemers & Van der Toorn, 2015; Leach, Bilali, & Pagliaro, 2015).

Although, one interesting idea that this puts forward is that if moral and immoral behaviours are determined by our social group and what group members feel are important to the society. Then this could suggest that there is no moral value at all to specific actions or overt displays of any kind.

For example, traditionally displays of empathy and helping behaviours are thought of as moral. Yet these exact same behaviours could be immoral or have different moral meanings depending on the social context they're used in. As well as this moral meaning relies on the relationship between the actor of the behaviour and the target (Blasi, 1980; Gray, Young, & Waytz, 2012; Kagan, 2018; Reeder & Spores, 1983).

Perhaps a clearer way to show this point would be, let's say a young man had fallen down three steps and he was hurting. Then someone else who saw it happen was trying to help him and was showing him a lot of empathy. Now if this helper was a close friend then this would have a close, very moral meaning, but if this was a complete stranger, then we could argue this helping is even more moral. Or if the helper had actually pushed the young man down the stairs, then would this helping be as moral as the friend helping?

I don't think so, so it just goes to show that social context does matter in moral judgements and deeming what behaviour is moral and immoral.

<u>Linking To Moral Grey Areas</u>

To wrap up the chapter, let me propose an idea about how this links to moral grey zones using a little relatable example. We all know that there are cultures within cultures, for example I live in the United Kingdom but not a single culture is monolithic. I am also a member of my university, psychology, writer, Medway and other smaller cultures within the UK.

Each of these cultures have a different social, political and religious context that influences my morality. Such as it might be perfectly immoral at university to cheat on a test and do any form of cheating, but within UK culture, I don't think many people would judge me too harshly.

I have never cheated on a test for the record. It is just an example.

Therefore, I wanted to show you a little example about how different people coming from different cultures (even subcultures) can have different ideas, beliefs and behaviours about what is moral in a particular situation.

Therefore, when a situation represents itself and

people from different backgrounds and social contexts come together and make different moral choices that other people might deem as morally grey. This could be an explanation as to why.

So that's a social or group-level reason for how morality forms, but how does the Self impact our moral behaviour?

WHAT IS THE MORAL SELF AND HOW DOES IT CONNECT TO MORAL GREY AREAS?

The next explanation for moral behaviour and I'll link this to moral grey areas later on, is the idea of the moral Self. This is an approach that expands the biological as well as evolutionary approaches that we talk about in different places in this book.

Since the moral Self proposes that within each of us there is an explicit self-awareness and autobiographical narrative that characterises our self-consciousness, and our moral self-views (Hofmann, Wisneski, Brandt, & Skitka, 2014).

In other words, it is argued that people have the self-awareness to view their actions as moral or immoral.

I know that probably seems like a lot of common sense but this is important to note in research.

Especially, as this seriously helps us to understand moral failures because if people are able to view themselves as moral or immoral. Then this raises the question of why the hell do people do immoral behaviours and risk seeing themselves as an immoral person.

Which we know from social psychology would lead to a decrease in self-esteem and that would have negative mental health implications.

Therefore, people are highly, highly motivated to protect their self-image at all costs because we want to see ourselves as good, moral people (Pagliaro, Ellemers, Barreto, & Di Cesare, 2016; Van Nunspeet, Derks, Ellemers, & Nieuwenhuis, 2015).

The benefit of seeing ourselves as good, moral people is it allows us to avoid self-condemnation, which makes us feel bad. And we're able to avoid this even when we fail to live up to our own moral standards.

How This Links To Moral Grey Areas?

Knowing that people want to avoid seeing themselves as bad people, it makes us wonder why people engage in any form of immoral behaviour. Even moral grey areas when there isn't a strict "good" behaviour to perform so chances are, some people will still see you as a "bad" person. Then this could have a knock-on effect on our own self-image.

As a result, research shows there are a range of strategies that people use to disengage any self-views they have from their morally questionable actions

(Bandura, 1999; Bandura, Barbaranelli, Caprara, & Pastorelli, 1996; Mazar, Amir, & Ariely, 2008).

Most of these strategies I think are rather basic but they are highly effective. This strategy involves you redefining your behaviour, as well as freeing yourself from any responsibility for what happens, excluding other people from the right to moral treatment, and not focusing on the impact the behaviour has on others.

These are only some strategies that people use to lessen the impact of morally questionable behaviour on their self-image.

In addition, we need to realise here that when it comes to a person's self-view of their own morality. This isn't about how other people see that person, this is all about how a person sees themselves in reflection of their internalised conceptions of the moral self (Aquino & Reed, 2002; Reed & Aquino, 2003).

More On The Moral Self

This results in a range of behaviour but one example is that this prompts people to simply forget the moral rules that they didn't adhere to (Shu & Gino, 2012). A favourite example that I can think of is if you ask any driver that has had a speeding ticket (this is an immoral behaviour because they broke the law), do any of them remember the rules about speeding? Or do they make up an excuse for their immoral behaviour?

I am honestly not having a go at people with

speeding tickets. I know 99% are just accidents and I might end up with one in the far, far future.

Anyway, some other behaviours this moral disengagement can cause include people fail to remember their moral transgressions (Mulder & Aquino, 2013; Tenbrunsel, Diekmann, Wade-Benzoni, & Bazerman, 2010) or people just dismiss other people who seem to be morally superior (Jordan & Monin, 2008).

If we go back to the speeding ticket example then some family members I know, they just dismiss me when I joke to them about speeding tickets and how they broke the law. Since I am technically morally superior because I have never sped before, but they have. Therefore, to protect their self-image, they dismiss me and my joke.

Thankfully, having a moral self-image can be a good point because it gives people a strong desire to show moral behaviour so people can continue to think of themselves as good, moral people (Ellemers, 2018; Van Nunspeet, Ellemers, & Derks, 2015).

On the other hand, it can get people to engage in symbolic acts that distance themselves from moral transgressions (Zhong & Liljenquist, 2006) or even makes them relax the standards they have about their own behaviour once they have shown their moral intentions (Monin & Miller, 2001).

Overall, a person's tendencies to be consistent, reflective and justified in relation to their own behaviours can be affected and guided by their moral behaviour. As well as their moral self-image can prompt people to adjust their moral reasoning, moral judgements of others and endorse moral arguments that help them to justify their own past behaviours whether they were moral or not (Haidt, 2001).

<u>Conclusion On Moral Grey Areas</u>

Since part of the reason for the creation of this book was a friend's off-the-cuff comment about their interest in morality and they are a massive Dungeons and Dragons fan, I want to nail home how this chapter links to moral grey areas using a DnD example.

I am utterly horrified with myself.

Anyway, in a campaign that I played in, there was a moral choice that was we could help a rebellion overrule the nobility by taking out the nobility's leader and only a few guards would die. Or we could do nothing and let the rebellion happen and because the leader was still alive, thousands of innocent people would die.

The choice was basically, do you kill one man to save thousands or do you do nothing and let thousands probably die.

For a lot of us that would be a very clear moral choice, but for some people this is a very grey moral area because you are still killing people. And even though you are killing a single person to save thousands, some people in this DnD game couldn't maintain their moral self-image because they were still killing.

Yet the majority of us in the party could easily maintain our moral self-image by killing one man to save many more.

I know that is a fictional example in the grand scheme of things, but if I have learnt one thing about good, committed players of DnD (something I am not) they take their game seriously. And I have no doubt that for some DnD players that would be a very, very real choice so that example might actually have ecological validity after all.

THE INTERPLAY BETWEEN THOUGHTS AND EXPERIENCES

Another principle that helps us to understand morality and it can be applied to moral grey areas too (something I talk about near the end of the chapter), is the principle that moral behaviours involve people having deliberate thoughts and ideas about what is right and wrong. As well as the emotional experiences and behavioural realities that people have influence their decisions to commit moral transgressions.

In other words, people do know and realise they are the ones in control of their actions and they realise they're behaving and thinking in ways that could be immoral.

In addition, the term "behavioural realities" comes up a few times in this chapter and I don't really think this is spoken about much within psychology, so I will define it for you all. Behavioural realities is the idea that humans gain meaning and understanding about the world through their social interactions and other social processes.

I have heard of this argument before but I haven't come across the term "behavioural realities" before researching this book.

Moreover, whilst this sounds like common sense, from a theoretical perspective, this is a rather new way of thinking. Since in the past, a lot of moral psychology was based on philosophical reasoning like how legal and political academia focuses on morality. Yet in this modern version of moral psychology, we focus a lot more on abstract ideas, deliberate decision-making of a person and general moral principles that come from a person thinking about the formal rules of a society (more on that later) and their consequences (Kohlberg, 1971; Turiel, 2006).

This perspective shift within moral psychology only started because of Blasi (1980) found the following and this is what the researcher said on page 1 of their paper:

"Few would disagree that morality ultimately lies in action and that the study of moral development should use action as the final criterion. But also few would limit the moral phenomenon to objectively observable behaviour. Moral action is seen, implicitly or explicitly, as complex, imbedded in a variety of feelings, questions, doubts, judgments, and decisions … From this perspective, the study of the relations between moral cognition and moral action is of primary importance."

Personally, I really like this way of looking at morality because it makes a lot of sense and it is ultimately true. Since we can talk about thinking processes, influences and what makes someone think or decide to act in a certain way all we want. Yet it is the action of a moral or immoral behaviour that is the only thing that really matters, it is the action that has consequences for people. So it makes sense why we should focus on the action and what leads to it.

Therefore, this perspective started to get even more popular and powerful within the moral psychology literature when Haidt (2001) wrote in their introduction about "moral intuition" as a relevant construct. Since this introduction looked at questions regarding what came first in moral acts, was it reasoning or a person's intuition. Then over the years, this has led to a lot of research with the results showing that there is evidence for both coming first (Feinberg, Willer, Antonenko, & John, 2012; Pizarro, Uhlmann, & Bloom, 2003; Saltzstein & Kasachkoff, 2004).

I know that doesn't make a lot of sense because how can reasoning and intuition possibly both come first in moral behaviour.

This can happen because our reasoning can shape as well as inform our moral intuition (which is a classic philosophical idea in its own right), but people can (and seriously do) justify our intuitive behaviours with post-hoc reasoning. This is Haidt's position.

And this is where things get interesting because these results suggest that there is an important interplay between a person's deliberate thinking and our intuitive "knowing" that helps to shape our own moral guidelines (Haidt, 2001, 2003, 2004).

Overall, we need to understand how our behavioural realities and our emotional experiences reflect our general moral ideas and principles.

How Do Emotional Experiences And Behavioural Realities Reflect Morality?

A lot of different researchers have looked at how our emotions and our behavioural realities impact our sense of morality. One of these examples can be found in evolutionary psychology and the associated value for the species of having moral guidelines.

Especially, as moral guidelines can help us to avoid diseases and contamination as sources of physical harm.

This is important to note because as I talk about in *Biological Psychology*, disgust is an emotional response that has evolved to help our survival. You can read the book to find out exactly how and why we evolved disgust but for the purposes of morality, disgust is an emotion that helps us avoid and keep a physical distance from a disgusting thing. Be it a person or a situation that might harm our survival chances.

Furthermore, this helps to explain that when we encounter a morally questionable or outright aversive situation, we are much more likely to avoid the situation in the future. (Schnall, Haidt, Clore, &

Jordan, 2008; Tapp & Occhipinti, 2016).

In addition, the social origins of our moral guidelines acknowledge and help to explain how the emotions of empathy as well as distress act as implicit cues that help us to decide who is worthy of our prosocial behaviour (Eisenberg, 2000).

Similarly, if we think about the emotions of anger as well as moral outrage towards people who violate moral guidelines then this helps us to understand which moral guidelines are important to us (Tetlock, 2003).

On the whole, our emotional experiences of empathy, disgust and outrage demonstrate that rather basic emotional states have direct consequences on our actions (Ekman, 1989; Ekman, 1992).

More On Guilt And Shame

I know we've already spoken about the role that shame and guilt plays in our morality but we need to explore these two emotions a little more. Since compared to the "primary" emotional responses that I mentioned in the section above, guilt and shame are "secondary" emotional responses that are a lot more complex and self-conscious states that we can't always see straight away (Tangney & Dearing, 2002; Tangney, Stuewig, & Mashek, 2007).

Instead these secondary emotional states are only really seen in humans with the vast majority of other animals not showing guilt or shame. Therefore, this allows other people to perceive the ability to experience these emotions and communicate the degree to which we consider someone to be human and worthy of moral treatment (Haslam & Loughnan, 2014).

Personally, I understand that paragraph was a little complex so I want to bring it back to a real-world example to help us understand it. If we think about secondary emotions, the paragraph above is basically saying, the more we see someone show guilt or shame or another secondary emotion, then we perceive them as more human and relatable. Then because we are more likely to act morally to people who are like us, we are more likely to act morally right towards them.

This could help to combat dehumanising tactics as well.

Moreover, similar to what we've learnt before, guilt and shame are "self-condemning" moral emotions that help to inform self-views as well as guide our behaviour towards hopefully changing so we don't have to feel these awful emotions again. The function of these emotions aren't actually to communicate our emotional state to others.

On the other hand, research has noted that a person can feel overwhelmed by their emotions of shame and guilt. This results in the person activating self-defensive responses that prevent them from improving their own behaviour (Giner-Sorolla, 2012). Also, this doesn't only happen at an individual-level, it can happen at the group-level with "collective guilt". Which is an experience that prevents intergroup reconciliation attempts (Branscombe & Doosje, 2004).

Finally, the main determining factor about whether guilt or shame impacts our moral behaviour is down to how we appraise the likelihood of being socially rejected and if we want to improve our behaviour so we can forgive ourselves (Leach, 2017).

Overall, at the end of this chapter, we should note that regardless of the emotion that a theoretical perspective focuses on, the theory shows that our moral decisions and our moral concerns come from the situations themselves, the emotions they evoke and people's experiences of the situation.

Something I built upon in the section below.

Linking To Morally Grey Areas

The content talked about in this chapter helps us to understand morally questionable areas, because it shows if someone makes a morally questionable decision once. Then there is a chance they will feel guilt and shame and they will be nervous about social rejection, promoting them to change their behaviour to avoid that fate. As well as to avoid making the same mistake again.

On the other hand, if a person doesn't care that much about social rejection because of their behaviour, then they will not change and they will keep doing the same morally questionable behaviour again and again.

In addition, if we outrage, empathy or anger because someone has violated our moral guidelines.

Then we might decide to act on these emotions because these basic emotions have a direct consequence on our actions.

Therefore, to use an interesting example from Dungeons and Dragons again, I remember in our game we had to decide if it was morally right to kill a powerful Lord who was killing children (yes, this is the same example as before). Yet there was a man in our party that was so outraged by this situation that he couldn't have cared less about killing this Lord because it meant saving the children.

Whereas others still had moral issues with the act of killing one person to save more, because killing of any kind is still morally wrong. As well as I highly suspect they felt less moral outrage or anger towards the Lord than this man did.

Of course, I understand this is a game so ecological validity of my examples is rather poor, but these gaming examples are just to get us thinking. And as I mentioned before, some people do think that the decisions they make in DnD are basically real-life decisions.

WHY MORAL JUDGEMENTS AREN'T ALWAYS BAD?

I decided to bring this into this section of the book because the fascinating topics you're going to learn about in this chapter, that draws on evolution, intergroup conflict and how morality can reduce the cost of these conflicts, all touch on a lot of grey areas.

And what I personally enjoyed about this chapter was it really focuses on explaining how morality is socially constructed and it shows you how this leads to but also decreases conflict.

This is a really fun morality chapter so please enjoy.

**

Before on The Psychology World Podcast, we've spoken a lot about different aspects of morality and how morality impacts behaviour. Yet we need to understand that judging other people and making moral judgements leads us into a moral grey area. Since we are always taught that judging others and their behaviour isn't always a good thing to do, and judging others' immoral behaviour can have negative consequences.

On the other hand, there is research evidence that suggests there are benefits to judging other people and this can have benefits for ourselves and our social groups.

Therefore, in this social psychology podcast episode, you'll learn more about this fascinating grey area of morality helping us to explain why people do good and bad things. If you enjoy learning about social psychology, morality and conflict then you'll enjoy this episode for sure.

Why Moral Judgements Aren't Always A Bad Thing?

We all realise that other people judge each other quite a lot, and sometimes this is just funny. I can't remember how many times members of my family have had a lot of conversations that make them angry because they're judging someone else's behaviour as utterly wrong. Even though it doesn't affect them in the slightest. My favourite example was in June 2024, me and some family members went to Oxford for a weekend and it was great. Yet these family members saw a trans couple and a particular family member was not impressed and they got really angry even though that couple had no impact on their life whatsoever.

I just found that family member funny.

Anyway, as you can tell, humans love judging each other and making a massive fuss over things that don't always affect them. This is a strict contrast to other animals because most animals don't judge each other this badly.

As a result, this led evolutionary psychologists to believe that our moral judgements help our social groups to avoid and even resolve conflicts whilst minimising the cost of each conflict.

This is an interesting idea that I rather like because we know moral judgements are centred round the idea that there are commonly shared rules for behaviour that we compare the behaviour of others to these shared moral values. For example, if we use the example of a young person pushing an elderly person to the floor then we would support the elderly person because our shared moral values tell us, it is wrong to push elderly people (or anyone else to be honest) to the ground.

In addition, moral values and these common rules for behaviour are, well, tied to a person's behaviour instead of their genetics and identity.

As a result, from an evolutionary perspective and I've spoken about this in different places, you might think we should only come to the aid of people who we are genetically related to or even more powerful or stronger people so they can help you as well in the future.

Yet in reality, as we know from other podcast episodes, this isn't how helping and moral behaviour work. Since this would actually increase conflict because if we all supported and went into conflict to defend our loved ones and the other side of the conflict did the same. Then this would result in long blood feuds that could go on for years or generations.

For instance, let's say back in 1901, you had two mining families in the same community and one day one of the families lost their favourite shovel. Then they blamed the other family for it. If all the family members rushed to the defence of their own family and they only showed moral behaviour to what is effectively the in-group and showed immoral behaviour towards the other family. Then this would cause a lot of conflict and if the shovel was never found or the families never settled their differences then this would spin out of control into a feud.

A type of conflict that could rage on for years or generations.

Equally, the same is true if we only helped or showed moral behaviours towards rich, powerful people who could help us in turn. Due to the power within a social group would become concentrated too much and this would only increase inequality and cause further conflict.

Overall, as you can probably guess, these side-taking strategies fail to minimise conflict within a group and these negative outcomes can harm the evolutionary fitness of the species over time.

How Rules Of Morality Help Minimize Conflict?

As a result, when we create rules of conduct,

better known as commonly known moral rules for behaviour. This allows the side-taking to become dynamic, so the most powerful person doesn't automatically win. As well as this conflict can become coordinated, because the sides of the conflict will be thrown out of balance and this helps to prevent any long-term feuds from forming.

Consequently, this type of dynamic conflict resolution is dependent on these moral rules of conduct being commonly known as well as widely agreed on within a social group.

And it is this commonly shared sense of right and wrong that helps to explain why people get really anxious about understanding what is right and wrong. Since people do not want to be seen as immoral and "bad" people, so this is why virtue signalling is a good way to publicly tell others what side of a conflict we are on and this allows us to understand what conduct rules people in the social group agree and disagree with.

Personally, I strongly believe this is difficult enough for neurotypical people but I know as an autistic person, this is even harder. And honestly, a lot of my psychological distress over the years has actually been from my inability to understand things like social rules and whatnot. I find it easy to understand the major moral and immoral rules, like do not commit a crime, because anyone can understand those points. Yet it is the smaller, more nuanced points about what is acceptable and moral within society that I struggle with and it causes me a lot of anxiety.

So if you feel the same way, even if you're neurotypical, then you aren't alone.

In addition, we have a lot of empirical evidence that people categorise behaviours into a moral or immoral category. It is just something that we do automatically and there is a benefit. Especially when it comes to amoral topics (things that have no right or wrong behaviour attached to them) because it allows people to enjoy a lot of diversity and freedom. These amoral topics are things like music choices, film preferences and haircuts.

And yet, people don't actually experience that much freedom when it comes to topics or issues labelled as moral or immoral. This means people have to rely on reading their social environments to truly understand or try to get a sense of what is moral and immoral behaviour, as well as understand which moral positions are up for debate.

Furthermore, until the "critical mass" or majority of a population agrees on a position about a particular topic then there is thankfully enough space to debate these issues regarding if they are moral or not. I really like that this happened in the 2010s in regards to same-sex marriage because the majority of people agreed it was moral in nature so most people continued to peacefully debate about the topic.

Then once a critical mass of the population agreed same-sex marriage was moral and slavery being immoral follows the same principles, people stopped considering this topic debatable. So people stopped listening and tolerating any form of social deviance within that topic and what is really interesting is this common position becomes "objectively right" in the eyes of the population.

Finally, before I wrap up with the conclusion, I want to stress how this critical mass idea helps to avoid conflict and prevents a conflict becoming too costly. Once a society or social group agrees on the moral rules of conduct then people compare other people's behaviour against those rules. So if someone does commit a moral transgression then we understand that that person was in the wrong and they are the one that should be socially punished for the transgression.

This stops a moral transgression spinning into a wider conflict because as a social group, we understand what happened was immoral and it never should have happened. This prevents the blame game and helps give different sides of a conflict power through the process of coordination and the conflict still being dynamic as I discussed a moment ago.

Therefore, there's no need for feuds or costly conflicts that would end up costing the social group a lot of precious resources that would decrease their evolutionary fitness and ability to pass on their genetics over time.

Conclusion

On the whole, when it comes to moral

judgements, the reason why we all focus so much on them is because we have a shared set of common moral values that we consider to be objectively right. Then these "right" moral and immoral behaviours help us to socially coordinate entire populations because these moral behaviours act as, effectively, traffic light systems for our behaviour. Allowing large groups of people to minimise any damage that will inevitably happen when conflict occurs.

And for better or worse, let's conclude with a smaller final real-world example, 2024 is a major election year in a wide range of countries that has the power to reshape the face of the world. So moral judgements, reducing conflict and minimising damage caused in conflicts could very well help us to understand why some people can be infuriated by politics and why others can be obsessed with it.

All because the hardest part of moral judgements is getting people to agree on which virtue signals to rally around in the first place.

HOW POWER CORRUPTS?

I definitely couldn't do a moral psychology book without touching on the corrupting influence of power and how it impacts morality. Now, you might be wondering how could power and its associated corruption possibly lead to someone doing immoral behaviours, or committing moral grey areas.

Firstly, we'll answer those questions in the rest of the chapter.

Secondly, the reason why I put this chapter of the book in the moral grey area section of the book, is because power and its corruption are one of the factors that can make someone do morally questionable behaviours. As well as outright immoral behaviours that have the potential to harm a lot of good, innocent people.

I really enjoyed this chapter so I hope you do to.

***

I highly doubt there is a single person that has

never heard of the idea that power corrupts people. Also, I think a quote I've heard from somewhere is "absolute power corrupts absolutely" I don't know where it came from but it's true for the most part. However, whilst a lot of people have heard about the corrupting influence of power, a lot of people don't know how or why power corrupts people. Therefore, in this social psychology podcast episode, you'll learn how does power corrupt people. If you enjoy learning about power, privilege and social psychology then you'll enjoy this podcast episode for sure.

How Does Power Corrupt People?

Typically, and I think this happens because it's easier to see, we think about powerful leaders and people in charge. Since it is generally these people that we see as powerful people who take advantage, take more than their fair share of resources and these people selfishly strive for even more control and power.

We typically think about powerful leaders as getting corrupted because the world is filled with dictators and so-called "strong man" leaders, so this allows us to easily see the damage that a powerful, despotic leader can cause.

However, we need to acknowledge that once a person has power then this can lead to corruption (typically moral corruption) and bad behaviour. So, how and why is power associated with corruption?

How Does Power Change Someone's Self-Perception?

The first way how powerful people can become corrupt is because their power changes their self-perceptions. Since philosopher Terry Price argues that powerful people engage in a mechanism known as "exception-making" where they don't believe the rules and laws of society apply to them.

This is a very, very easy source of corruption and I can easily think of five, ten, maybe even twenty politicians and celebrities that fit this category.

In addition, it's worth noting there is research evidence that the more powerful a person is, the more they focus on their egocentric needs and desires, as well as they were less able to see other people's perspectives.

Personally, I think this is really interesting because if we draw on Piaget's work from developmental psychology, then children before the age of 7 work in the exact same way. They focus on their own needs and desires and they often fail to understand or see the point of view of others. Which looking at some celebrities and politicians, I think calling them 7-year-old children is an insult to children.

Anyway, this "exception-making" is even more problematic for people in positions of authority and power who could exploit the people they are in charge of.

Power Gives Someone Privilege

The second reason why power corrupts is because powerful people have a lot of resources that they can use to their benefit. Therefore, this allows the powerful people to achieve and experience things that less powerful people can only dream of. For example, fine dining, fast cars, penthouse apartments and so on.

In other words, powerful people get special treatment and this can lead to corruption because powerful people can buy their way out of trouble.

We can all see this relatively easily because the Criminal Justice System does operate on two tiers, because powerful people can hire the best lawyers, they can bail themselves out of whatever trouble they find themselves in and they can throw whatever money they need to make it go away.

I'm sure we can all think of famous politicians and celebrities that have done this in the past few years.

In addition, powerful people can intimidate and threaten other people too. I see this repeatedly in films, books and I sometimes use this in my Bettie English Private Eye Mysteries, when a character says "Don't You Know Who I Am?". Then after a powerful person does this, it's normal for a less powerful person to back down or they support that powerful person and benefit from their alliance. In the short term, this tends to benefit the person but longer term this can make the person powerful themselves but it can corrupt them too in the bitter end.

As a result, to make it clear, a powerful person threatening others can lead to corruption because it shows they can bend others to their will, manipulate them and subjugate them. All of these are immoral behaviours.

Why Doesn't Power Have To Corrupt?

So far, we've looked at what can make someone become corrupt and this connects to moral grey areas too. Yet being a powerful person doesn't have to make you corrupt, because there are a lot of wonderful, kind and highly influential celebrities and politicians, so power does not always corrupt.

The difference between these corrupt and uncorrupted powerful people is "socialised" power, this is power used to benefit others, and "personalised" power, this is power used for personal gains, according to a range of leadership scholars.

Therefore, some people argue the best way to stop power corrupting someone is to keep them humble, because it's important that powerful people are humble when evaluating their behaviour objectively. Since these powerful people need to realise that their power isn't their right, instead it is given to them. Also, their power can be fleeting, and it's important that the people closest to the leader (like their inner circle) actually keep the leader accountable to stop them becoming corrupted.

Conclusion

Overall, in this podcast episode, we learnt that power can corrupt people because it changes the powerful person's self-perceptions so they don't believe laws and rules apply to them. Also, it gives them privileges other people don't normally have so they can get out of trouble easily in addition to threatening and intimidating others.

At the end of the day, we all need to know (especially leaders and powerful people) that it is our obligation, our duty, our moral responsibility to use our power to benefit others. We should never abuse any power we have because this can be illegal at times and it is always immoral behaviour that has the power to harm others.

Something we should never ever do.

PART FOUR: REAL-WORLD MORALITY

MORAL PSYCHOLOGY

5 SIGNS OF PSYCHOPATHIC PERSONALITY

To kick off this next section of the book, I wanted to start us off by looking at a type of person who has no morals, no morality and only serves themselves. Whilst I continue to say that psychopaths are scary as hell to me, they are brilliant to talk about in a morality book. Since they are such a violent contrast to "normal" people who have a moral centre.

Therefore, whilst this next chapter doesn't focus implicitly on morality, it still provides us with a valuable glimpse into the mind and personality of psychopaths. And we can draw out inferences regarding morality from what we find in psychopaths.

Enjoy.

***

Psychopathy is a great topic because it captures the imagination as well as the vast majority of psychopaths are male. But of course women do have psychopathic personalities too, and whilst I talk more about psychopathic personality in my Personality Psychology and Individual Differences, I wanted to tell you about the signs of psychopathy. And all of them are extremely interesting.

5 Signs Of Psychopathy

Superficially Charming

This is what everything thinks of when they think of psychopaths because they are charming to get their own way. Since unlike you and me, we tend to be transactional in our relationships because that's fair and the right thing to do. Whereas psychopaths will charm their way without self-restraint to get what they want.

You might notice a person with psychopathic personality as being too slick and overly nice to work their way towards their goal.

But going back to us being transactional, the psychopathic personality is not.

Instead they are instrumental and only use people for what they are good for. Then without a clear reason or cause, they can turn cruel, cunning and even dangerous. Meaning you might realise a person with the psychopathic personality's style is to belittle and seduce others to get what they want. And not the normal style of bonding with others and helping them as much as they help you.

<u>Deceitfulness</u>

As psychopaths always feel the need to be on top and their lack of ability to bond with others as well as they have distorted self-esteem. Psychopaths will lie, cheat, rationalise their actions and twist the truth to such extreme degrees that reality is unrecognised to any objective people.

And this is what I want to stress. Because it is natural for people to lie, cheat and do what psychopaths do to a lesser extent. But psychopaths will always go an extra ten miles in their deceptions because they have to do it for themselves due to their distorted self-esteem, their inability to bond with others and always be on top.

<u>Boredom and A Need For Simulation:</u>

This point connects to the one below and psychopaths have shallow emotions as well as a high stimulation-seeking drive ([Personality Psychology](#)) that means they get bored quickly. Resulting in, when combined with their need to constantly seek out stimulation, psychopaths being quick to take chances and take part in risky behaviours.

Again if we compare the "normal" person to psychopaths, we all engage in risky behaviours from time to time, but if we're sensible we at least think about it first. Psychopaths don't weigh up the risks and think about it logically. They just go for it because it's fun and thrilling and they need the stimulation.

Shallow Emotions:

What makes this next characteristic so strange is how charming psychopaths can appear. Since psychopaths can have "good" conversations with people about their lives and they can appear to be present and engaging in the emotional conversation.

Then the psychopath can just change the conversation in an instant and that's when people start to realise how shallow their emotions are and how much they don't care. For example, you might be talking to a psychopath about a family member that you loved dearly dying last month. Then the next second the psychopath could change the conversation completely.

Of course, even if we didn't want to be in the conversation because we didn't know this person and the person telling us is a stranger. We've all been in these sorts of conversations forced on us by others. We know to let the other person finish, say supportive words then maybe change the conversations.

Psychopaths don't understand that because of their inability to bond with others

A History of Shady Conduct

To wrap up this look at characteristics of the psychopathic personality, we need to acknowledge that with psychopaths having no moral centre and a high stimulation-seeking drive. It is hardly surprising to hear that sometimes their behaviour can catch up with them but sadly it is normally far too late for their victims by this time.

For example, in the book Decoding Madness, the author describes a case where a psychopath was admired by their supervisors because of his effectiveness in sales. But then the risky behaviour of their fraud and killing got revealed.

All in all, psychopaths will engage in risky behaviours and take chances to commit crimes because it's thrilling, exciting and it feeds into their stimulation seeking needs.

Conclusion:

Overall, I hope you enjoyed this personality psychology episode as much as I did. Psychopathy it isn't a good topic to experience first hand, but I do enjoy looking at it from afar so I hope you enjoyed it.

Personality Psychology References

Lettieri, R (2021). Decoding Madness: A forensic psychologist explores the criminal mind. Prometheus Press. Chapters 6 and 11

Workman, Lance. "Interview: The memory worrior." The psychologist; The British Psychological Society 25. (2012): 526-529.

Kiehl, K (2014). Psychopath Whisperer: The science of those without conscience. Broadway Books.

MORAL PSYCHOLOGY

WHY ARE WE DIVIDED ON WHAT MAKES A GOOD SOCEITY?

Our next chapter is a lot of fun to be honest because it definitely deserves to be here in the fourth section of the book. Since this chapter really does focus on society and what is happening in the real-world with political polarisation and different ideas and concepts that impact every single level of society.

As well as in case that doesn't automatically sound like something that has any connection to morality, we need to remember that morality is about what is deemed to be right or wrong behaviour.

This chapter deals a lot with why people simply don't agree with what is morally right and wrong.

Also, this chapter easily would fit in the third section of the book, because there is an argument for Social Justice and Social Order worldviews as an explanation for what others consider morally grey areas.

Yet I am digressing, this is a brilliant chapter and

it is very applicable to our lives.

***

You only need to look around, turn on the news or read anything on social media to know that we are very divided about what happens in a good society. This heavily connects to our sense of morality and what each of us deems to be right or wrong in a given situation. Therefore, in this social psychology episode, you'll going to be learning about why are we divided in our moral judgements about what makes a good society, how to foster more constructive conversations and the difference between Social Justice and Social Order. If you enjoy learning about social psychology, some political psychology and moral psychology then you are in for a treat.

Why Are We Divided On What Makes A Good Society?

It should hardly come as a surprise to any of us that western societies are becoming more and more polarised. Since the US, according to the 2023 Edelman Trust Barometer, is severely polarised and the UK, France and the Netherlands are in danger of becoming severely polarised. And as someone who lives in the UK, I firmly agree with that conclusion. Then there are other countries like Ireland, Canada and Australia that show concerning signs that they could be polarised in the near future.

Of course, there are a lot of different reasons for this and it is a very complex and difficult area to fully understand. Although, there are some trends that we are certain about because there is a growing division in our societies about what makes a good and just society and what is the best way to go about this.

Personally, there is nothing surprising or even shocking about this because you only need to turn on the news to see the truth in this argument. Since the very idea of what makes a good society is constantly subjected to normative theorising that has been going on for thousands of years. Therefore, this has led to a very, very wide range of perspectives and ideas that are often in conflict with each other. For example, nationalism or internationalism, conservatism or socialism and so on.

In addition, these differences and divisions in our beliefs about what makes a good society can create cause for concern. And what I find interesting about this "cause for concern" is that it isn't actually about the opinion per se (because we do need a wide range of opinions and ideas) but the cause for concern actually comes from the inability of each side to understand as well as have constructive conversations with the other. This is even more important when we consider how different sides don't talk to each other constructively about shared challenges.

Leading us to our next question.

How Can We Understand These Different Perspectives On The Common Good?

One way of understanding these different and often competing beliefs comes from Iceland et al.

(2023) because these sociologists propose that there are two basic moral worldviews that are termed Social Justice and Social Order. Then in their new book *Why We Disagree About Inequality: Social Justice vs Social Order.* These two worldviews are actually both opposite of each other and they are very distinct ideas behind our morality, wisdom of the past, human nature and social change.

And Social Justice and Social Order relate to how people think and respond to inequalities like racism, gender and income and more.

As a result, we can apply Social Justice and Social Order to the polarisation of the western world because we can understand people's worldviews by looking at these two concepts. Also, this is useful because this helps us to create a sense of mutual understanding that can hopefully foster a want for opposite sides to talk to each other instead of whatever they normally do. I don't even have a word for what opposite sides do.

Maybe screaming, shouting and threatening each other?

How To Understand Social Justice and Social Order?

Now we're going to understand these two worldviews by looking at how they apply to different areas of our social world. And this certainly gets interesting and applicable.

Individual And Group Morality

Thankfully, research like Greene (2013) and Haidt (2012) shows that regardless of someone's political orientation, the want to care for others is deemed important. Then if we draw on Moral Foundation Theory (Graham et al., 2009; Haidt, 2012) which proposes that people have moral foundations around individualising (like caring for others and protecting others as a central concern) and binding (like putting group cohesion and social order above all else) moral foundations. The sociologists argue that Social Justice and Social Order worldviews have distinct moral foundations.

For example, someone who has a Social Order worldview focuses on group loyalty and respect for authority whereas someone with a Social Justice worldview focuses on putting *care for the vulnerable*.

On the whole, Social Justice and Social Order impact morality differently because different aspects of individual and group behaviour underpins what people believe is morally right and wrong differently.

<u>Fairness and Equality</u>

Similarly, everyone regardless of their political beliefs care about fairness, but depending on whether someone has a Social Justice or Social Order worldview, they conceptualise fairness differently.

Due to Iceland et al. (2023) argue that someone with a Social Justice view tends to understand as well as measure fairness by the outcome. Whereas someone with a Social Order view focuses on processes.

In practice, this means that these different views correspond with a difference in how each group views how equality is construed. So someone with a Social Justice view stresses and focuses on the equality of the outcome, and inequalities of the outcome is the result of discrimination. Whereas people who have a Social Order view focus on equality of opportunity with variation in outcomes being down to a person's individual differences in their effort, preferences and talent levels.

I would add my thoughts to what I think about those definitions but I don't want to make this book any more political than it needs to be. Yet I do like these arguments because they're logical, based in evidence and you can apply them to everyday life.

<u>Responsibility and Choice</u>

Now this is going to be interesting because people with Social Justice and Social Order views focus on very different things when it comes to choice and responsibility. Since Iceland et al (2023) describe that a person with a Social Order view understands choice and responsibility in terms of opportunities and options. Whereas someone with a Social Justice view understands freedom (to make choices) in terms of influence and power.

Therefore, whilst it is true that both worldviews focus on how able people are to make choices, they're rather different in how they conceptualise the freedom that people have to make these choices.

As a result of Social Order believes people should have the freedom to pursue any opportunities for their success and well-being. Whereas Social

Justice believes people should be free from oppression and discrimination.

Now you think that these views are basically saying the same thing, but when we consider that capitalism in the strictest and most traditional senses often involves exploiting others and oppressing them to become successful. This is why typically Social Order is seen as a more capitalist approach and Social Justice is more socialist.

<u>Social Change</u>

I've definitely saved this one until last because this is going to be the most fun for me and it is going to be the most divisive, so let's play.

Regardless of whether a person believes in Social Justice or Social Order, everyone agrees the world can be improved. The problem is these two worldviews have completely different ideas about how to change the world and what needs to change in the first place. There can be overlap and shared ground but in my experience, this is rare.

Social Order sees social change as something that needs to be done very slowly, in small increments because they believe it is the nature of complex systems to operate by means of "trade-offs" instead of solutions. So Social Order believes whenever we socially change we don't create a solution, we trade something for another and there are advantages and disadvantages of this change.

On the other hand, Social Justice prefers rapid and extensive change that helps to improve the world.

In addition, both perspectives are associated with different views and opinions about the past and a culture's traditions. Since someone who believes in Social Justice is associated with almost a rejection of traditions in an effort to move forward and create new, better solutions for problems. Whereas Social Order looks to the past and traditions to solve problems.

Which I always think has "interesting" results.

<u>Conclusion</u>

At the end of this podcast episode, there are two main points I want to mention.

Firstly, this relates to morality because whether we believe in Social Justice or Social Order ultimately affects how we think, we act and what we view as morally right or wrong behaviour in society. Then this has implications for our own moral behaviour, moral judgements and more that I've spoken about before on the podcast.

Finally, I really want to stress this point because I want us to not only learn about psychology and human behaviour. I also want us to take away lessons and use them in our own personal lives. Therefore, we need to use this knowledge about worldviews to inform our thinking, our moral behaviour and our own moral tribes. Due to we need to understand that both Social Order and Social Justice should be on an equal footing and once we do this, we can understand how the world looks from each side of an argument. Hopefully helping us to talk to the other side instead of shouting, screaming and yelling at them.

Something that achieves nothing at all.

We don't ever have to agree with an opposing viewpoint but if we are willing to listen, learn and understand them. Then maybe we can help make the world a better place that is a bit more respectful, a little less polarised and a little less dangerous for all of us.

HOW DOES LYING EVOLVE ACROSS THE LIFESPAN?

When it comes to writing a psychology book that covers so many facets of a massive topic, you often have to fight with yourself about where to put different chapters. The overall aim is to help create a reading order that is interesting too, engaging and easy on the reader.

In that sense, I could have put our next chapter that focuses on the lying behaviour of young children, older children and adults into the second section of the book. Since age and other developmental psychology factors do influence moral behaviours, but I decided against that.

Also, I could have put this chapter in the Grey Area section of the book, because this shows that lying isn't always bad, but it isn't always good.

Yet I settled for the fourth section because

parents and children exist in the real world, and come on, who doesn't like talking about how moral children and parents are towards each other.

This is going to be interesting to say the least.

***

It might be common sense that the type of lies and lying behaviours that young children use are very different from adults. Although, generally-speaking, we aren't sure why this happens and we aren't sure on the nuances of these lying behaviours across different ages. Let's fix this in today's episode. Therefore, in this social psychology podcast episode, you'll learn how lying evolves across the lifespan including how the types of lies and the complexity of our lies change over time. If you enjoy learning about social psychology, deception and developmental psychology, you'll love today's episode.

Brief Examples Of Child-To-Parent and Parent-To-Child Lies

To give us all a fresh understanding of the different lies children and adults tell, I wanted to explain why these are important to look at as well as I'll give you a few examples of each.

Firstly, generally, all of us lie at different points in our lives and we lie in different situations where it seems to be the better choice compared to the truth. Even though we know lying is normally considered a socially immoral behaviour that we shouldn't do, but come on, lying is a lot more complicated than right or wrong.

Therefore, it's important to look at the differences in the complexities and types of lies that children and adults tell, because this helps us to understand the nuances of lying behaviour. As well as we can understand why lying isn't a simple matter of right or wrong.

Here are some examples of Child-To-Parent Lying

- "He/ She started it!"

Everyone in the world has probably told this lie as a kid because the child does this because they don't want to be punished so they lie and get rid of any responsibility of hitting their friend or sibling first.

- "I'm too sick to go to school today"

This lie can happen for a range of reasons, including not wanting to see a bully at school and they're too ashamed to tell their parents, or they don't want to see a teacher because they haven't done their homework.

- "But Dad said I could"

I think I've told this lie a fair bit as a kid because it worked and it was so easy. Since this lie is about appealing to the other people who the child has never approached or asked permission or said it was up to the other parent to decide.

Examples of Parent-To-Child Lies

- "You'll get arthesis in your fingers if you get clicking them"

That won't happen but it gets the child to stop the behaviour the parent finds annoying.

- "You'll damage your eyes if you keep watching TV"

Interestingly, this might have been true back in the 1950s because TVs emitted a lot of radiation, but this isn't true today.

"The Elf On The Shelf is watching you so Santa knows what you're doing"

I don't even need to explain this lie.

How Lying Develops Over The Lifespan?
Why Is The Lying Of Young Children Naive?

Compared to the lying of older children and adults, the lying behaviours of young children are rather naïve. Since the lying of older children is more complex and more "knowing", and older children lie for a wide range of different reasons and like adults, older children lie to serve themselves.

However, this is much harder for young people to develop. Since it isn't until the age of four that children develop Theory of Mind so young children assume that their parents will take whatever they say literally and instantly understand what they mean. At this point in their lives, young children don't understand that their parents or caregivers will probably have a different perspective.

This connects to one of my favourite topics in developmental psychology and this is egocentrism. Since young children aren't able to take other viewpoints and they can only focus on their own personal rewards, punishments, goals as well as dreams. They don't understand other people's reactions or aren't "able to put themselves in their shoes".

A personal example of this is really bad. Yet when I was about 10 years old or younger, I had a massive interest in Lego so my favourite Godmother brought me a Lego Pirates of The Caribbean set that was on the market for £9.99 back in the day. And I liked the present but tactlessly said in front of her and my parents "I knew I would get this because it's cheap,"

How ungrateful and how egocentric of me!

I feel bad for saying it and I get nowadays it was an awful thing to say, but it goes to show how tactless children can be.

On the whole, it's important to realise here that young children can't understand the concept or value of "white lies" and how they can help protect another person's emotional welfare.

Equally, there is a benefit to young children being egocentric. The benefit is they can be awful liars because they don't understand or care to learn about the times, places and ways to make a lie successful. As well as young children don't realise the importance of hiding their true feelings by covering their tracks.

Like I should have done when I was really young.

What About The Lying Behaviour Of Older Children?

Nonetheless, when the child gets older, their lying behaviour becomes more and more like their parents because they learn from getting trapped by their parents' teaching them how honesty is the best policy and the times when the older child has tried to hide the truth from their parents.

Furthermore, older children become more "cognitively able" to copy and learn from their parents' lying behaviour. As a result, if we care to indulge the idea that lying is a skill (which I personally think it is, whether that is right or wrong is another debate entirely) then it's like a child's lying skill matures as they age. This helps to make the older child as effective at lying as their caregiver, who is often hypocritical.

Why Lying Isn't All Bad In Children?

Additionally, whilst society generally regards lying as an immoral behaviour, a lot of experts think of lying as an important step in child development. Since lying shows the child is learning how their minds are separate from their parents, they are a person in their own right and they sometimes need to lie to their caregivers.

Of course, there are extreme cases of the need for lying behaviour. Like I needed to lie as a child for my own safety, but thankfully I no longer need to do that. Then they are more normal and less extreme cases, for example a child needing to lie about eating the last of the ice creams to avoid getting into trouble.

Also, lying, like saying "no" is important for the child's development of boundaries and so the child understands they should have different boundaries to their caregivers. And they don't need to always agree and be the same as their caregivers.

There are some wider social benefits of lying behaviour for children which we'll look at now.

How Lying Becomes More Complex In A Social World?

Another reason why lying becomes more complex and "improves" is because we live in a socially interdependent world so children do grow past the normal developmental stage of self-absorption. This leads to older children being better at telling lies, and it improves their ability to mirror their parents' motives.

In other words, the reasons for the lying becomes more polished, mature and complex.

For instance, when children are young, they lie to get what they want so they might lie to fulfil an emotional need or a physical one. This happens because as you can expect, children have no authority so they are completely dependent on the caregiver.

Therefore, young children need to find ways to incentivise their parents to give them what they need.

However, as the child ages and their cognitions and understanding becomes more complex, their motives become more complex too.

As a result, children are able to lie more tactically

and more manipulatively if required.

How Parents Lie To Protect Their Children?

At the end of the day, I think it is fair to say that a lot of lying behaviour, at least between a caregiver and a child, comes down to protecting the other. Since great, well-meaning parents will lie to their child and I don't think this makes someone a bad parent, because it is normal to want to protect your child against learning about things that they aren't old enough to understand without feeling threatened or in danger.

Of course, as a person from a certain background, I acknowledge I am missing so many nuances here and some parents will sadly stop their children from learning about things because it threatens the parent or the parent's so-called morality. For example, parents stopping their children from learning about gender equality, sexual orientation, racism and so on. Thankfully, these are just the minority of parents.

Anyway, in this context, I am talking about parents preventing their children from learning about murder, terrorism and similar scary things.

Also, I accept there are lots of selfish and bad reasons why parents lie to their children but I don't have the time or space to write about them here. And honestly, that stuff is just heartbreaking. If you really want to check out those bad reasons then please check out the references at the end of the book.

Therefore, these protective motives that make a

parent lie can relate to a range of motives. Firstly, a parent might keep their child safe by hyperbolically increasing the dangers that they would be vulnerable to. Like, "don't eat all those sweets or you'll throw your guts up,"

Secondly, parents could tell a lie to shield their child from a hurtful disappointment or a harsh reality that will probably overwhelm them. Like, "Daddy's working," to explain to a child why they won't see their dad on their birthday.

Thirdly, a parent can lie by placing a limit or disciplining a child whilst taking care not to shame their child. Or by avoiding badly timed or counter-productive arguments. As well as parents can lie to maintain some control over their child's destructive or rash impulses.

Finally, and this is my favourite reason because we all do it, parents lie to children to increase their self-esteem, confidence and happiness by telling them about Santa being real, praising them for some "interesting" creative painting or whatever the child cares to call it. Since these lies prevent the child's feelings from getting hurt.

I'll explain how parents and children can lie to each other out of love and other reasons in the next section.

Parents And Children Use Deception

In our final section, I really like this content because I have lied so much to my parents and wider family over the years, because I have had no other choice. Yet I have also lied for a wide range of other reasons, so I really do appreciate and understand the different reasons why children and parents lie to each other.

Firstly, parents and children lie to stop the other one from worrying about something that the liar doesn't think is actually that serious. A child might lie about bullying at school because they think they can handle it alone without the parent. Or a parent might tell a child that their other caregiver has went away for work for a few days instead of telling them they went in for a quick routine operation.

Secondly, both children and parents lie to avoid disappointing each other. Like a parent might not tell their children about not getting a job promotion, or a child might tell their parents they passed an exam when they actually failed.

Thirdly, and this is a massive one in my experience, children and parents lie to maintain peace and harmony. This was why I couldn't afford to tell my homophobic family about me being gay because that would have caused so much disharmony within the family system. Thankfully, it wasn't as bad as I feared in the end but it was still… interesting.

Penultimately, we all lie to protect the self-image of another person. I remember a few Christmases ago, there was a member of my family that looked rather large and when they sat down, we all thought this person was heavily, heavily pregnant. Of course, I know you shouldn't say things like that so I lied to them and said they looked great. Thankfully, they realised their weight a few months later and now they've become a more average weight and they couldn't be happier with their life.

Finally, it's important in any relationship that the two or more people involved are independent and autonomous from each other. Therefore, parents and children can lie to each other so they can establish distance, a sense of personal control and maintain privacy from the others. I remember last year at the time of writing that I was getting extremely annoyed at my parents because we have a Ring doorbell and they would always want to know what I was doing when I left the house. They thought it was funny but let me tell you, it seriously fucked me off.

In reality, I think at this time I was heading off to therapy for some trauma and abuse, but I lied to them easily enough. I just said a psychologist was letting me do some work experience with her for an hour on a Tuesday morning.

Even now I love how well that lie worked because it was such a stupid lie if you think about it.

Conclusion

Whilst in this podcast episode, I have explained a lot of benefits and reasons about why both children and parents lie to each other. There can be valid, good and maybe even moral reasons that excuse the generally immoral nature of lying to loved ones and lying more generally to other people. Yet I do not want to leave this episode on that note.

We still need to teach our children that lying isn't something that they should do all the time, and I still strongly believe we should teach them that lying is bad.

However, we need to acknowledge that lying can be useful and moral if it has good social and ethical value that helps us to protect our own feelings and the feelings of those we love.

BYSTANDERISM AND AULTRISM

I decided to take the next three chapters from *Psychology of Relationships: The Social Psychology of Friendships, Romantic Relationships and More* for three main reasons. Firstly, I flat out love bystanderism because it is such a counter-intuitive topic that really makes you question morality and human behaviour. Secondly, these topics directly connect to morality because morality is concerned with helping behaviour and doing the right thing.

Thirdly, the next three chapters show you why people don't always help others and why they might engage in immoral behaviours. Since if we think about not helping an innocent person in distress or trouble or who's injured. Then this is immoral behaviour by societal standards and yet so many people don't help.

Why not?

That's the focus of the next three chapters. Especially, because Bystanderism and Why People Don't Help contrasts really well with the Altruism chapter. It shows a wide range of fascinating human behaviours within three chapters.

Enjoy.

Bystanderism

In this chapter, the studies will talk more about Bystanderism than me, but it will be interesting.

Bystanderism is also known as the Bystander Effect is when someone is less likely to help if there are other people around.

The Bystander Effect, I do find interesting because why do people not help when you can clearly see that someone needs help.

In everyday life, there are thousands of examples of the Bystander Effect.

Here are only a few examples and I bet that all of us would like to think we would help but, in reality, I bet none of us would help, or only the best of us would.

- You see a man being chased down the street by a group of three men who look intimidating or threatening. The man being chased clearly needs help and is terrified for his life.

- You're stuck in traffic and you see an old lady walking past with heavy shopping bags, and you know that she's going to fall.

- You're on a busy train and you see a young girl getting bullied by a group of mean girls.

And there are thousands of more examples demonstrating the Bystander Effect.

Personally, I find it interesting because as a society we are bred to be helpful and the best we can but when it comes down to it. Barely any of us are actually helpful to complete strangers.

For the case studies, I'll do a combined critical thinking section.

Darley and Latane (1968):

In this study psychology students took part in a conversation with other students over an intercom system.

In round 1 each participant was to present their problems. Round 2 was to comment on what other people had said and round 3 was for free discussion.

In reality, all the other people heard over the intercom system were recordings.

The future victim spoke first in the discussion telling the participant that it was hard to adjust to the new city and he was prone to seizures under stress.

In round 2, he started to have a seizure and asked for help then went quiet.

Then the subject was timed to see if they went to find help and after being debriefed, they filled in a series of questionnaires.

The results showed that the number of bystanders does increase the response time as when it was the victim and participant 85% responded to the emergency and it took an average of 52 seconds to respond.

Whereas only 31% of people responded when it was them, the victim and four other people with it taking them on average of 166 seconds.

In conclusion, the participants were in conflict about whether or not to help because they didn't want to overreact and destroy the experiment but equally they didn't want the shame of not helping. This can be explained by diffusion of responsibility as with there being more people there were more people for the responsibility to be psychologically distributed.

<u>Latane and Darley (1968)</u>

Whereas in this next study students were placed into three groups and all were asked to fill out a questionnaire and after a while, the room began to fill with smoke.

One group was when the participant was in the room alone.

Group two was when the participant was in the room with two other people. These people were asked to act indifferent and ignore the smoke.

The last condition was when the participant was in the room with two other participants.

Results showed that when alone 75% of the participants reported the smoke.

When with two other people only 10% reported the smoke and when in condition 3 only 38% reported the smoke.

In interviews, participants thought the smoke was strange but wasn't sure if it was dangerous.

In conclusion, when faced with an ambiguous

situation people tend to rely on the reactions of others and are influenced by them. This can lead them to interpret the event as not dangerous and a phenomenon known as pluralistic ignorance.

Critical Thinking:

While both studies were effectively controlled as they both had several experimental groups so we could see the effects of Bystanderism in different contexts as well as with several different numbers.

Both studies lacked ecological validity because if we take the intercom study for instance. In a real-world situation, you can see other people's expressions to a situation and these expressions amongst other things play a role in deciding whether to help or not. Therefore, this could affect the results because this could have led to an increase in the response time or a decrease.

MORAL PSYCHOLOGY

WHY PEOPLE DON'T HELP?

In the last chapter, we looked at the Bystander Effect and three factors behind Bystanderism.

So, in this chapter, I wanted to investigate the topic of why people don't help in more depth because Bystanderism isn't the answer to everything.

Rationality of Not Helping:

To answer this question, Bickman (1972) ran a study where the participants were led to believe they were in an experiment with two other participants/confederates.

Subsequently, the participants heard a bookcase fall on top of one of the confederates, and the participants believed the other confederate could or couldn't help the person.

Also, they heard the other confederate interpret the event as an accident or not.

In short, as a participant would have heard the bookcase fall on another person and if it was an accident or not, as well as if you were needed to help rescue the person.

The results showed participants were a lot more likely to help if the confederate deemed it to be a definite emergency and they couldn't help them.

This makes sense because if someone is trapped; it wasn't urgent and you weren't needed to help. Chances are you aren't going to help because you're not needed.

And yes, I can hear the numbers of readers saying "Yes I would still help,"

I agree I want to think that but chances are we won't.

<u>When Do Numbers of Bystanders Increase Helping?</u>

I quite like the study below because in psychology we hear a lot about the negative sides of the social group (Social Psychology 3rd Edition) and the Bystander Effect.

Therefore, I always love studies that turn the current research consensus on its head.

Since we think the number of Bystanders only decrease helping, but it can increase helping in certain situations.

Greilemeyer & Mugge (2015) conducted an experiment where they told students they needed 1 or 4 people to do an experiment. As well as the participants believed they were alone or 10 other people had received the request.

<u>The hypothesises were:</u>

- If one person is needed the number of bystanders should decrease helping as supported by Latane & Darley (1968)
- When others are needed, the more bystanders there are, there should be an increase in helping.

Their results showed the participants thought helping made 'less sense' when one person was needed but many were available. As well as when many were needed and only 1 was available.

This was caused by the diffusion of responsibility in the first scenario.

Whereas when the opposite was true when many people were needed, and many were available. This increased helping.

Again, I think this study has a lot of real-world applications because if multiple people are needed to help. Then what's the point of one person trying?

Also, I would love to think that I would still try and chances are I probably would. Yet it is still interesting to consider.

A Final Study:

Lastly, Harari, Harari & White (1985) studied rape scenarios on a university campus to see if men alone or men in groups would help.

The results showed men in groups overwhelmingly helped. Probably due to feeling safe and the norm is to help.

Critical Thinking:

Nonetheless, the study was far from perfect because helping is naturally strong in a natural setting. Since humans are inclined to help others.

You'll see in the next chapter on Altruism how true that can be sometimes.

Additionally, there was no discussion of ethics in the study because these weren't briefed, and informed consent wasn't obtained before the study.

Furthermore, when someone cries rape, you know its an emergency so the generalisability of the findings might not be as high as you think it is.

Due to the results of the study can only be generalised to situations that are clearly an emergency.

On the positive side, participants who thought they would have to talk to the participant later helped faster.

In addition, the number of confederates had no impact on this. (Gottlieb & Carver, 1980)

Lastly and perhaps the most interesting finding is public self-awareness reverses The Bystander Effect.

I talk a lot more about self-awareness in Social Psychology. Yet I think this is an interesting finding as it could mean the way to get more people to help others, could be to make them more aware of themselves in these situations.

Since if people know they're being watched, and let's face it judged by others, for their actions then it might make more people help others.

For example, if a person was walking in a street and they saw an elderly lady fall over and no one, including the elderly woman saw that person, then there's a chance they would avoid the situation, and hope someone else would help.

However, if that person thought about the negative judgements other people would be giving them for not helping. Then maybe, just maybe they would help.

It's an interesting idea to think about.

MORAL PSYCHOLOGY

ALTRUISM

Prosocial behaviour is an interesting topic in psychology because it's difficult to say why human show the behaviour. Especially, when we show altruistic behaviour.

This behaviour is when we help others even when the behaviour could harm us.

For example, let's say you're walking through your street and you see a gang of people with knives beating up a stranger, and it's clear that the stranger will die without your help, and you run over to help the stranger. Even if it could result in your death.

That's altruistic behaviour.

Yet WHY do it? When there is such a high risk of danger and it goes against many psychological rules.

Such as evolutionary theory states that we wouldn't help because it would threaten the chance of us reproducing and passing on our genes to the next generation, so it goes against evolutionary theory.

Thus, psychologists are divided on the why of

this particular behaviour.

As some believe that we show altruism for egotistical reasons. For example, you would attack the gang so you could feel good about yourself and you become a local hero. Increasing your social status in the local community.

Then other psychologists believe that humans are capable of true altruism, so you helped that stranger because you just wanted to. It was the right thing to do.

Personally, I'm more cynical so I believe in the egotistical reason.

What Factors Can Determine If Altruism Occurs?

- Personality (Rushton et al., 1986) and situational factors can increase helping. For instance, if you have a helpful personality then you are more likely to help others as well as if the situation promotes helping then you are more likely to help. One example could be if others are helping then you are more likely to help in that situation compared to a situation where everyone is simply walking past. (See Bystanderism for more information)
- Machvavellism is the willingness to manipulate others for gain. As excepted as Machvavellism increase, helping behaviour decreases.

- Empathy- as expected the more empathy a person has the more likely they are to help someone.
- Moral reasoning- people who reason more tend to demonstrate a higher level of empathy and altruism.
- Religiosity- if you're religious and if your religion promotes helping others then you are more likely to people to serve your god or Faith.

However, this isn't always true because if you would insult or offend your religion by helping a particular someone. Then you are less likely to help someone. For example, if it's an extremely devoted Christian then helping a gay person would be unthinkable since they're a sinner.

- Having positive role models- Scloeder, Penner, Dovido and Pilivin (1995) showed that people who witness more altruistic behaviour from role models tend to be more altruistic themselves.
- Similarity- if the person who needs help is like you then you are more likely to help them.
- Culture- as collectivistic cultures focus more on the needs of the group, they are more likely to help than individualistic cultures. (See Social Psychology for more information)

Belief in A Just World:

This is the belief that the world is fair and that people get what they deserve and generally the belief in a just world is likely to prevent people from doing wrong or failing in moral duties. (Hafer, 2000; Sutton and Winnard, 2007)

However, these beliefs can increase the chance of people not helping when they don't feel obligated to help. (Balbert, 1999; Stelan and Sutton, 2011) As well as people who believe in a just world will often blame the victims and only help people if they think the person deserves help.

Reciprocity:

Another two important factors that determine if prosocial behaviour will occur is reciprocity and equality. As a result, reciprocity is the obligation to return in kind what another has done for us. For example, if I helped you with a psychology assignment at university, you would feel obliged to help me with an assignment if I was stuck on it.

Reciprocity is important for humans because it has social benefits as well as human societies endorse reciprocity and to some extent it can be considered a social norm.

As seen in Kanz and Woolcoli (1976) who sent Christmas cards to strangers and found an increased response rate when the sender had a higher status. Hence, supporting the idea of reciprocity being endorsed and encouraged in society.

Moreover, reciprocity can be broken out into two types. The first is direct reciprocity where you are directly reciprocating the help you got. Like, *I help you, you help me*. Whereas the second type is indirect reciprocity. This can be described as *I help you, someone else helps me*.

Interestingly, this type of reciprocity is important for reputation building, morality judgements as well as the term social karma.

I use this a lot in my business because I create a lot of useful content on The Psychology World Podcast for free, and this helps a lot of people. Then someone buys one of my books or shares the content with someone else.

Again though, I don't plan this but I work on the assumption that if I'm useful to people then my reputation will built along with my social karma.

Something else that determines if we reciprocate for the other person is our willingness to request or accept help. This is often predicated on the ability to return the kindness. For example, if you wanted help on a university or work assignment after recently helping your psychology friend on their assignment. You would probably be rather willing to ask them so this predicts the reciprocity should be high. Whereas if your friend wasn't a psychology person then this would poorly predict their ability to help you after you helped them.

Equity:

Reciprocity and equity go hand in hand because equity makes sure each person benefits proportionally to their need or contribution. For instance, it would be extremely unfair if you were in a group and you did the majority of the work, but the other people benefited as much as you. considering you did most of the work! This is where the idea of proportionality comes in.

Whereas equality argues that everyone gets the same amount regardless of the effort or work they put in.

The whole point of this section is to explain when people feel they under benefited from their contributions, they rightfully feel anger. (Hassebrauk, 1986) Whereas when people feel they over benefited from their contributions, they feel guilty. (Austin, McGuin & Susmich, 1980)

Mood:

Speaking of feelings of guilt, a person's mood is very important in determining whether or not they help a person because positive moods have been shown to increase helping in a wide range of settings. For example, in charity donations, helping peers and donating blood. (Isen, 1999).

Whereas negative emotions or mood may or may not increase helping as a result there is some evidence of feelings of guilt, whether it's from the perception of not being able to help or another reason, are followed by reparative behaviours. This is where the person focuses on making themselves feel better rather than helping the victim.

What Can Increase the Chance of Being Helped?

When it comes to helping behaviour there are certain characteristics that can increase the chance of being helped. For instance:

- Age- the younger you are the more likely it is that people will help you. This could be linked to evolution as the young are more fertile so by saving them we are increasing the likelihood of them reproducing and ensuring the survival of the species.
- Gender- woman are more likely to receive help than men. (Bruder- Maltson and Hovanitz, 1990)
- Attractiveness- the more attractive you are the more likely it is that you will be helped (Witson and Dovidio, 1985)

Interestingly, research has shown gender plays into prosocial behaviour in a surprising way because it is males who help strangers more instead of women. Whereas women are more likely to help family members compared to men.

From my personal experience, I completely agree with the research because it was my mum who helped out the family members the most after two deaths in the family in two years.

Kin-selection Theory:

This theory was proposed by Hamilton (1964) as

an extension of evolutionary theory and he stated that we help others to increase the chances of our genetic material being passed on.

So according to the theory:

- Relatives will be the target for helping behaviour as they will have more of our genetic behaviour than other people.
- Closer relatives would be helped more than distant ones as they will have more of our genetic material.
- Healthier and younger people would be helped more as they are more likely to reproduce and pass on the genetic material.

However, I personally must highlight a few problems with this theory:

- How can humans detect genetic material in strangers?
- Why do humans help complete strangers?
- Why do humans help elderly or infertile people as they won't be able to pass on genetic material?
- Finally, why do humans help homosexuals as they are unlikely to pass on their genetic material?

If the theory can answer those questions, then I'll probably believe in the theory a bit more.

<u>Madsen et al (2007):</u>

UK students and South African Zulu were asked to provide a list of genetic variable people. Like: mother, siblings and grandparents.

Then they were asked to take up a painful position like sitting on a chair with your back against the wall and legs and thighs at right angles.

They were asked to hold the position for as long as possible and time equalled a payment; £1.50 for 20 seconds for UK students and food hampers for the Zulu people; for the recipient. There were five trials in total each for a different person. Like: themselves, mother, brother, cousin and a local charity.

Results showed that subjects were more prepared to maintain the position for people they were related to. For example, they held it for longer for themselves over their parents.

This was transcultural.

In conclusion, kinship plays a role in moderating altruistic behaviour.

Critical Thinking:

While, this experiment was a cross-cultural study, so we know that the behaviour is a part of the behavioural trend and possibly universal.

The study has low ecological validity as in the real world I doubt this situation would ever be used or happen. Therefore, it's questionable about whether we can apply the findings to the real world given how artificial this scenario was.

Empathy-Altruism Hypothesis:

Batson et al's theory states that people help others have real concern and if another person has empathy for another then they will help.

As I said though, I'm cynical so I have complete faith in this theory, not.

Batson et al (1981):

44 female psychology students took part in a 2x2 experiment involving them going into a room and watching a recording of Elaine who was being shocked at random intervals. From the first shock, it was clear she found them very unpleasant.

From the second trial out of ten, the subject was allowed to help her by taking her place.

The 4 conditions that made up the groups were: easy vs difficult escape wherein the difficult escape they believed that if they didn't help her they would have to continue to watch the situation.

In the easy escape condition, they believed they could just walk away.

Low vs high level of empathy- this was done by everyone completing a questionnaire on values and believes and Elaine's was done beforehand then her questionnaire was shown to the subject so they could know if Elaine was similar or not to them. As the study claimed that increased similarity means increased empathy towards the person.

The results showed:
- Easy escape/low empathy condition- 18%
- Easy escape/ high empathy- 91%
- Difficult escape/low empathy- 64%
- Difficult escape/ high empathy

In conclusion, when the level of empathy was high the desire to help was altruism not egoistic and ease of escape no longer had an effect when the level of empathy was high.

Critical Thinking:

While this study has strong internal validity as it effectively measured what it intended to.

It does have several ethical concerns as the students weren't protected against the possible psychological harm and deceit used in the experiment.

Forgiveness:

Whilst this isn't traditionally thought of as a type of prosocial behaviour, sometimes it can be, since forgiving someone can be in the best interest of the self, the social group and society.

Therefore, forgiveness is when you stop feeling angry towards or seeking retribution against someone who has wronged you. since forgiveness can heal retaliation (McCullough, Pargament & Thoreseen, 2000) as well as there are physical and mental benefits to forgiving someone. (Coyle & Enright, 1997; Witerhet et al, 2001)

Linking to relationships, we have all had to forgive a friend or loved one at some point or another, and the more committed you are to a relationship, the more likely you are to forgive someone. (Finkel, Rusbult, Kumashio & Hannon, 2002) I know it's extremely hard sometimes!

On the other hand, there are limits on the power of forgiveness because despite how committed we are to a relationship. The worse the offender and lack of remorse, the harder it is to forgive. As well as ruminating about the offence someone has done against you often leads to anger instead of forgiveness.

Finally, prosocial behaviour makes us human because humans, unlike animals, frequently act in prosocial ways towards non-family members. As well as if you know about Social Psychology then you know rule following, obedience and conformity are often portrayed as highly negative but these are for the most part positive. This includes helping behaviour because it is a result of social norms and conformity that we help others.

MORALITY AND THE BASICS OF CULT PSYCHOLOGY

It turns out that I can never resist the urge to talk about cults and cultic behaviours because I think they are fascinating, they are scary as hell and I suppose a small part of me wants to try and protect people from becoming involved in cults as much as possible. Idealist I know but my book *Cult Psychology*, was still a lot of fun to write.

So why talk about cults in a moral psychology book?

I wanted to do this because morality is concerned with the concept of right and wrong, and cults are typically always doing the wrong behaviour by our social norms. For example, a cult involves a leader forcing people to give up their freedom, autonomy and identity to force them to worship the cult leader.

That isn't moral behaviour.

Then if we think about some famous cult examples, like the mass suicides that some cults perform and the cult leader forcing members to take part, that is extremely immoral behaviour.

So why do cult leaders and their followers perform these immoral actions?

That's the focus of the next two chapters, because in this first one, I'll give you the basics of cult psychology so you understand cults better. Then in the next chapter, we focus more on cult leaders and the tactics used to control others. Again, controlling others is an immoral behaviour.

Overall, the entire point of the next two chapters is to show you some immoral behaviours in the real-world and why they occur. So keep reading and enjoy, and if you want to learn more about the psychology behind cult behaviour definitely check out, *Cult Psychology,* available wherever you got this book from.

***

Cult psychology draws on so many great areas of psychology from clinical psychology to social psychology and more. Also cult psychology is critical to learn about because not only is it extremely interesting but it helps us to recognise and protect ourselves against cultic influence. So let's learn more about the basics of cult psychology.

Basics of Cult Psychology: Extract From Cult Psychology (COPYRIGHT 2022 Connor Whiteley)

As much as we all want to dive into 'proper' cult psychology, we really need to learn the basics first.

And unlike a lot of psychology basics, the basics of cult psychology are very fun and worth a read.

But first, why is it important to learn about cult psychology?

Personally, I would love everyone to learn about cult psychology because by learning about cults, how they work and how to defend ourselves. This can help us keep ourselves, friends and family safe from cultic influence.

<u>Vulnerability and Recruitment:</u>

When it comes to cults, there is a very sad truth. No one joins a cult willingly. No one willingly chooses to give up their freedom and replace their lives with a superior leader that controls them.

Instead people are recruited into cults.

Now I understand if you're a bit confused by the distinction (I know I was at first). But the difference between willingly joining and being recruited by a cult is there's a lack of informed consent.

Another way to illustrate my point would be to imagine yourself wanting to join a cooking club. You love cooking, you love making friends and this cooking club doesn't try to influence you or control you. Then it's likely you'll willingly want to join it.

However, if this cooking club tries to influence you, use manipulation tactics and start brainwashing you. Then you aren't going to willingly join that. Instead you're been manipulated and recruited to join the cooking club.

As the treasurer for my university's baking

society in 2020/21 that was a very scary idea.

So, how are people recruited by cults?

It mainly comes down to vulnerabilities due to a cult can easily learn someone's vulnerabilities and use them against them. As well as sadly everyone has different individual vulnerabilities. No one is perfect and this brings me back to the important point about learning cult psychology and tactics. Therefore, in case anyone tries to use these tactics and vulnerabilities against us. We can hopefully recognise and deal with the situation.

Some of these vulnerabilities are situational and others are internal. For example, the death of a loved one, moving to a new country, area or city, being on the Autism Spectrum, high hypnotisability and having strong active imagination are all vulnerabilities.

Interestingly, if a person makes excessive use of hypnosis, medication, drugs and other activities. Then this can actually induce an altered state of consciousness.

Overall, all these vulnerabilities increase a person's susceptibility to being recruited into a cult. And sadly chances are if someone does have a lot of these vulnerabilities then it is rather likely they will be recruited into a cult given the chance.

Unless the person has strong critical thinking, media literacy and a good supportive social network around them to keep them grounded.

In addition, what media literacy means is a person's ability to critically analyse, thinking and evaluate the source of the information.

<u>Example of Media Literacy</u>

Personally, I'm not afraid of making myself sound like a snob (I'm a very normal person in real life) but this is why I only read and trust two or three media outlets in the UK. As well as I don't read tabloids and they're very manipulative and I don't trust their reports.

Mainly because there was one article in a British Tabloid in 2021 trying to get people shocked and horrified that a woman spent £6,000 a month on living bills. At first, I agree that seems a lot and no one should spend that much money, surely?

Then I evaluated what the tabloid was saying and it mentioned the woman paid so much a month for a professional subscription. Just like psychologists, doctors and lawyers have to.

Overall, my point is this tabloid wanted to make people annoyed and shocked for no reason. Because this woman was almost certainly a high flying professional on at least £50,000 a month so to her and her partner £6,000 is probably not a lot.

<u>Other Risks:</u>

In addition, to the risks above, there are a number of risks that can increase a person's vulnerability to recruitment by a cult. For instance:

- Trauma
- Phobias
- Alcohol or drug problems

- Learning or communication disorders
- Unresolved sexual issues

A quick note on these other risk factors is trauma, learning or communication disorders and unresolved sexual issues can possibly all relate to a person's want for support and community. As well as sadly if a person is isolated and doesn't have a good social support network then a cult with all those members can seem rather tempting.

Furthermore, in more recent years, there has been new risk factors that we'll look in various ways later in the book. Thus, some 21st century risk factors are:

- Internet addiction
- Lack of touch, social distancing and isolation
- COVID-19 pandemic
- Severe economic disruption
- Increased time online

Overall, if a person is in a vulnerable state then they can fall for one of these many techniques and be recruited into a cult.

What Is a Cult?

After talking about the various vulnerabilities people have and how cults recruit people into their ranks. We need to define what is a cult?

I want to say up front that the word cult shouldn't be used lightly because as we'll see in a moment cults can have horrific consequences to the members. As well as a group shouldn't be called a cult because of its unorthodox beliefs.

For example, a new branch of a religion that believes in a more liberal approach to the religious teachings isn't necessarily a cult. Simply because of its unorthodox beliefs.

What a cult is, is it's usually authoritarian in nature and it's led by a person who has complete or almost complete control over its followers. And this all comes down to influence.

<u>Cult Influence and Control</u>

To be able to control a person, a cult must influence them and recruit them into the group. With the aim being the cult influence is designed to replace a person's identity with a new one.

Now, this is done in a lot of different ways and some of these tactics we will look at in the book.

However, each type of cult has different ways of acting and conducting themselves. Some types of cults are:

- Political
- Religious
- Large group awareness training
- Self-help
- Multilevel marketing
- Commercial
- Conspiracy theory
- Labour/ sex trafficking
- Mini-cult (family/ one-on-one)

Building upon this, different cults do things differently. For example a political cult focuses on influencing people through political means and drawing on their political beliefs. Whereas a self-help cult would draw on a person's desires for self-improvement and to better themselves.

Moreover, one of the biggest problems with trying to recognise influence is we're being influenced every single day and we're use to it. I talk more about persuasion and social influence in my Social Psychology book. But we're constantly being exposed to influence, and this can make it difficult to detect.

Here's some examples of sources of influences in everyday life:

- Business
- Psychotherapy
- Politics
- Religion
- Educating
- Media
- Relationship
- Parenting

Nonetheless, I do need to say influence can be positive and helpful. As seen in psychotherapy, educating and parenting. But influence can be detrimental too. For instance in some parenting, relationships and religion.

HOW DO NARCISSISTS USE CULT LEADER TACTICS?

Continuing with our look at immoral behaviours in cults and narcissists, this is a fascinating chapter allowing us to see how cult leaders manage to pull off their immoral behaviours and keep followers under their control.

Just writing that last sentence made me feel uncomfortable because cults get up onto some extremely immoral behaviour, and I think it is beyond scary that there are methods, techniques and tactics that allow people to control and influence others.

I hope you enjoy the next chapter as much as I did writing it.

How Do Narcissists Use Cult Leader Tactics?

People high in narcissism have very high self-esteem but it comes from an insecure place. Meaning when their self-esteem is threatened, this causes them to become defensive and hostile (and engage in immoral behaviour).

As a result, they try to influence and control others around them so other people don't threaten their self-esteem.

In fact, the tactics narcissists use to control and manipulate others have a lot of similarities with cult leaders.

Leading us onto the topics below.

Act Larger Than Life

It shouldn't surprise you that narcissists and cult leaders both act larger than life. Since this seems them seem wonderful with innate goodness and they have special knowledge that nobody knows about. As well as they believe that nobody is above them.

For cult leaders, this makes sure the cult members don't question them.

For narcissists, acting larger than life means the people around them don't threaten their self-esteem because they're special and gifted with secret knowledge.

Questioning Is Not Tolerant

In cults, questioning is horrified because if you question the cult, its leader and its purpose. Then you will quickly become ostracised and socially excluded. Because in the eyes of the cult, you've committed heresy, since how dare you question the all-knowing leader!

As a result, narcissists can use the same trick because if they exclude or become rageful at people who question them. Then the people around them will know not to question the narcissist and this gives the narcissist some level of control over their behaviour.

Additionally, the reason why questioning is so terrible for narcissists is because this is a direct threat to their unsecure self-esteem. Because you could be implicitly implying in your questions that they're wrong and they don't know what they're talking about. This will almost certainly decrease their self-esteem.

Lies Are Repeated So Often

With the cult leader being in such high regards and never ever being in the wrong. This means they repeat their lies so repeat that the cult member believes it.

Therefore, narcissists can do the same. All they need to do is keep telling those around them the same lie and how wonderful they are, and overtime the people around them will start to believe it as the truth.

Their Righteousness Justifies the Means

Continuing on with the fact that the cult leader is perceived to be righteous and almost divine in some cases. It should come as no surprise, and you only need to look at some cults in the past 50 years to see this, that cults take part in some activities that normal people will shunt. Because it goes against their moral and ethical code.

Yet the reason why the cult members don't have a problem with this is because the cult leader says it's fine. Thus, the cult members believe it must be okay because the leader said so.

Additionally, if we think about it narcissists do some immoral behaviours at times. For instance, shouting, screaming and occasionally attacking people that threaten their self-esteem.

But if the narcissist has control and influence over those around them then these other people will most probably deem their behaviour as reasonable.

Meaning the narcissist's righteousness justifies the end.

<u>Independence Is Punished</u>

A while ago, I was reading an article on the psychology of cults on Psychology Today and I remember this point being raised in one way or another. The writer of the article showed the point perfectly because when she was invited into a cult and she wanted to socialise. The cult leader moaned at her because *she was inferring with God's time.*

Consequently, cult members are meant to be dedicated to the cult and they are meant to be one with the cult.

Otherwise, they are punished for their independence. This punishment can include social exclusion and ostracism and people prefer to keep social bonds even bonds that are bad for us. (Psychology of Relationships)

Finally, narcissists can control others around them using this trick because if the narcissist punishes someone for not being devoted to them. Then this could cause the narcissist to have stronger influence and control over this person.

MORAL PSYCHOLOGY

HOW LYING DESTROYS SELF-ESTEEM?

When looking at the consequences of immoral behaviour, I've noticed that people always tend to focus on the victim of the immoral behaviour, and not always the teller or person doing the immoral behaviour.

In this book so far, we've focused a lot on why and how the person commits immoral and moral behaviour, but not the effects of the behaviour on them.

That changes in our next chapter.

Since this next chapter, we look at a fascinating psychology article I wrote looking at how lying (an immoral behaviour at most times) destroys our self-esteem.

Something else I liked about writing this article is I was very much in a critical-thinking mood when it came to this study's methodology, so please enjoy.

I know I did.

***

Everyone lies at times, be it a small or large lie. For example, a loved one might wear an ugly dress or trousers and you tell them, they look lovely. That is a little white lie, but it is still a lie. Whereas a friend might invite you out or to a major event, and you say you're busy when you aren't. That is also a lie. Lying is normal to some extent, but how does lying impact our mental health and self-esteem over time. In this social psychology podcast episode, you'll learn how does lying destroy self-esteem by looking at some 2023 research. If you enjoy learning about social psychology, deception and mental health, then you'll enjoy today's episode.

<u>Why We Need To Look At Lying?</u>

Whilst we understand that people lie for all sorts of reasons and some people even lie daily, we typically only think about the "victim" of the lie. For example, when I found out a particular person lied to me once, I was deeply hurt, troubled and I experienced a lot of negative emotions and thoughts.

Yet no one ever thinks about the effect of the lie on the teller or Liar.

If I look at my own behaviour, before my breakdown in August 2023, I had to lie daily weekly or daily just to stay alive because of my abuse and trauma. I had to lie about my life, who I was and who my friends were just to stay alive and have a roof over my head. It was this constant lying and that partially led to my breakdown.

That's why I wanted to do this podcast episode. As well as we'll be focusing on the finding of Preuter et al. (2023) that was published in The British Journal of Social Psychology. And just for the sake of clarity, this was a Dutch team that ran four experiments on the effects of lying. As well as the basic hypothesis of the experiments was that because we all consider lying to be generally immoral, lying would lead to decreases in self-esteem and an increase in negative emotions.

How Does Lying Affect Self-Esteem?
How Lying Leads To Decreased Self-Esteem And Increased Negative Emotions?

Therefore, the first experiment done in this study was an online survey where the participants needed to read about different other-centred and self-centred moral dilemmas. Then the participants had to answer questions about whether they lied or told the truth, the last time they were in a similar situation.

For clarity, self-centred dilemmas are lying about yourself, like lying about how amazing you are in a job interview. Whereas other-centred dilemmas are about lying about other people. For instance, lying about how lovely and slimming that ugly new dress is that your best friend has just bought.

Afterwards, the participants were rated on the negative emotions of regret, discomfort, nervousness and unhappiness, as well as their self-esteem was determined by questionnaires.

Personally, I think it's interesting they chose to measure lying by getting the participants to remember when they had been in a similar situation before. I suppose this is the only real way to do it, but there are methodological flaws here. For example, the social desirability bias, because none of us like admitting to immoral acts and we don't like to remember we lie, which is the next point to be honest.

Anyway, the results showed that 41.6% of participants had lied during the self-centred dilemmas and 45.5% had lied for the other-centred dilemmas.

Interestingly, the self-esteem and negative emotion scores were clearly different between the participants that had lied and had told the truth. Therefore, these results suggest lying does cause a decrease in self-esteem and an increase in these four negative emotions.

Remembering A Lie Reduces Self-Esteem and Positive Emotions

In addition, in the second study, the researchers used a similar methodology as before but instead of dilemmas being presented, the participants had to present the dilemmas themselves. Here, the participants had to come up with situations where they could lie or tell the truth. Then the researchers determined the negative and positive emotions shown by the participants.

Again, the results showed that when participants remembered a time when they had lied, they showed a decrease in self-esteem and less positive emotions compared to participants who had remembered a time when they had told the truth.

I don't know why but I am in a massive critical thinking mood today, and I know in reality this is rather impractical because of budgets, expertise and how long this takes. Yet I would have liked to see some other data besides self-reported measurements, because I can't help but think whether it is possible participants were reporting or wanting to be sad, because they committed a socially immoral behaviour.

And not because they actually felt bad.

Also, it is possible the participants might be feeling negative because of the situation itself, the people in the situation or other contextual factors that aren't necessarily about the lying itself.

I know I'm probably being nit-picky but they are valid points.

Effects of People Lying More About Themselves Than Others

Personally, I flat out love replication in research because it is a very good research practice, as well as I truly love method triangulation. This is where you use data from different research methodologies to support your findings and this increases the credibility of your results.

Therefore, the entire point of the third study was to replicate the results of the first two experiments using a diary research approach. Here, the participants were asked to keep track of all their lies for a single day in a diary, as well as they were asked to write down what the lie was and why they had done it.

I might preferred a long time period for this diary approach so we could see how lying, its effects and its motivations change over a time period, but the results are interesting enough.

The results showed that 22.1% of participants told a self-centred lie whereas 8.5% told an other-centred lie during this single day. Also, 69.7% of people didn't lie at all that day.

Overall, the results showed that people who had lied that day had lower self-esteem and felt less positive about themselves when compared to people who told the truth.

Effects Of How Often Do People Actually Lie

Now, I am very interested in this final experiment because it uses one of my favourite research approaches of all time. In this study, the researchers used a longitudinal design so participants could track their lying behaviour and self-esteem over a course of five days.

Again, I think five days is a little short because I know from personal experience, there are some weeks when I needed to lie a lot and there are some weeks when I just don't need to lie. I think this short timeframe might have meant some of the nuance of this behaviour was lost, but equally, if you need your study going for too long then dropout rates increase. And let me tell you, dropouts are extremely annoying.

On the whole, the results showed that 22% of participants had lied every day during the study and

19% of the sample said they didn't tell a single lie on any of these days.

How Does Lying Impact a Person On The Day They Told It?

Finally, the fourth experiment replicated the findings of the other studies and the researchers found that on the day someone tells a lie, the self-esteem of the liar decreases as does their positive emotions.

Nonetheless, something I thought was interesting is when the researchers analysed the results of the diaries, they found their self-esteem was lower than the day before. That isn't surprising or very interesting. Yet this is interesting when we consider that a person who lies doesn't generally have low self-esteem beforehand, so self-esteem isn't a reason or causal explanation of lying.

Instead it is the act of lying itself that decreases self-esteem, and it is the combination of these four experiments that supports lying as a causal factor for decreased self-esteem.

Conclusion

At some point in the near future, I absolutely have to convert all my research and notes on the forensic psychology of deception into a book. Yet until that day comes, you should know that generally people are terrible at detecting lies, but we need to acknowledge that even if we get away with a lie, there are consequences.

Therefore, at the end of this social psychology

episode, I want to mention to people that lying might be a brilliant way to get out of a party or social event, we don't want to go to. Also, lying to a friend about their ugly new dress or clothes might be a great way to maintain the friendship and make our friend feel great.

Yet it has its costs.

If we want to feel good about ourselves then maybe lying isn't the best idea. So whilst the truth might hurt ourselves and our friends, it might be worth it considering the toll lying takes on our long-term psychological well-being.

Just a thought.

CONCLUSION: WHY WE ALWAYS NEED TO BE MORAL IN PSYCHOLOGY AND WHY THERE ARE NO EXCUSES IN THIS BOOK

Out of all the various chapters in this book, it is this final one that I have had the most ethical and moral problems with myself. Since the original research and comments I was going to write about clashed with my own morals so badly, because it was an argument about whether clinical psychologists should be allowed to discriminate against clients on the basis of Free Speech and Free Expression.

We absolutely do not have the right to discriminate at all no matter what the law says.

In addition, what I am referring to here is the various legal loopholes, especially in the United States of America, that allow discrimination to go unchecked on the basis of Free Speech. For example, the US Supreme Court Ruling between *Creative LLC Versus Elenis (2023)* that allowed the website to legally discriminate against a same-sex couple because homosexuality and same-sex marriage went against the beliefs of the web designer.

Then I was going to comment on how this ruling could apply to mental health professionals and deal with how different professionals can deny people mental health support through the use of Free Speech, Free Expression, Conscience Clauses (see *Ward versus Polite, 2012 for more information*) and a few more legal ideas.

But I will not do that.

I will not even remotely imply that any form of discrimination is okay even if the law says it is okay for mental health professionals to deny people who need support, the critical psychological care they need.

I will not stand for that and I do not want to even remotely be associated with this debate, because it is outrageous.

Therefore, I want to remind everyone that even though in this book, we have covered a lot of different morality topics and what influences our morality. None of these topics, factors nor influences should ever be used as excuses for acting immoral.

Just because you've been socially influenced, for example, that doesn't excuse you being immoral and giving someone shocks until you believe you have killed someone.

I know this sounds idealist, but there are no excuses when it comes to morality. Especially, in psychology and even more so for the applied areas.

My background is in clinical psychology because I say there is an unofficial mandate within the field. It is the duty of a clinical psychologist to improve lives, decrease psychological distress and help clients develop more adaptive coping mechanisms for their mental health difficulties.

If we do not do those three things to the best of our abilities then we have failed as a professional. So if we allow ourselves to act immoral towards clients, let alone discriminate against them then we haven't just failed ourselves and our clients. We have failed our profession.

And that is outrageous.

What Is The Path Forward For Morality Within Clinical Psychology?

I know the vast majority of people reading this book would never think about being discriminatory towards our clients or anyone in society, but it is something we always need to be aware of, because we should always try to do the right thing in any situation. Even if our personal and professional beliefs and morals conflict.

As a result, when it comes to clinical psychology, the concepts of doing good, avoiding doing harm towards our clients, being fair and respecting the freedom of our clients is absolutely important for guiding our behaviour in the therapy room and beyond (Beauchamp & Childress, 2019).

Since it is our duty as mental health professionals to make sure all our clients regardless of who they are have equal access to services and they are free from discrimination within our services. That is in the APA's General Principles and the NASW's Ethical Principles.

Yet this isn't always as easy as it sounds.

Therefore, it is beyond critical that we have educational programmes that help, educate and make sure all mental health professionals are prepared to work with clients, regardless of their background and their social identities. Even in the face of the professional having religious or moral concerns about their relationship (APA, 2013).

Furthermore, Barsky (2023) recommends we have professional consultation and supervision to help professionals with any potential struggles they have between their personal and professional morals and beliefs. Since we do need frank discussions about ensuring everyone has equal access to the mental health care they need.

And more importantly, we need laws, policies and professional practice procedures that help to reinforce this so it becomes a critically ingrained part of our profession.

Personally, I definitely think the above paragraph is aimed at the USA, because a lot of this research focuses on the US. Yet this is important for all countries to consider, because I am glad that the UK's NHS and the UK's clinical psychology programmes do place a massive emphasis on diversity, inclusion and trying to make sure everyone can have equal access to different services.

Of course, the NHS isn't always successful and there are massive gaps for improvement, but it is a focus and there are amazing people trying to move heaven and earth behind the scenes to improve things for people. And I respect the hell out of those people.

Finally, because this chapter is serving the purpose of a conclusion as well, I want to stress one thing about applying morality to the real-world. I have a minor French obsession at times because of the culture, language and some friends I've had over the years and the French do have a brilliant line for morality.

Whilst there is no evidence the last Queen of France, Marie Antoinette actually said "let them eat cake", it is a very useful line for morality. Since she was believed to have said this line in response to hearing the plebs moaning about their lack of bread and they were starving.

Therefore, Marie Antoinette knew that cake was more expensive than bread as a kick in the teeth for the plebs.

In modern times, this expression is used to show disrespect and disdain from a person of privilege towards people who lack privilege.

On the whole, this is useful for morality because it doesn't matter if you're a psychology student, professional or just someone interested in why humans do right or wrong behaviour. We all need to try and make sure we never have a "let them eat cake" attitude towards other people even when the lives these people live conflict with our own morals and beliefs.

We should treat everyone we meet with respect and dignity because everyone deserves that.

Especially within psychology, because when we work with our clients, we truly do have the power to improve lives, transform them and make people realise there is an entire world of possibility and happiness out there. But we can only work with people if we put our personal beliefs to one side and we give our clients the respect they definitely deserve.

Since there might be factors or situations that influence our moral behaviours, but at the end of the day, it is always up to us to decide how we want to behave or how we make up for our actions.

So if you take anything away from this book, please let it be, always try to act morally because it's powerful, it's beneficial and it certainly helps to make the world a better place.

REFERENCES

Ajzen, I. (1991). The theory of planned behavior. *Organizational behavior and human decision processes*, *50*(2), 179-211.

Ajzen, I., & Fisbbein, M. (1974). Factors influencing intentions and the intention-behavior relation. *Human relations*, *27*(1), 1-15.

American Psychological Association (APA). (2013). Serving a diverse public.

American Psychological Association (APA). (2017). Ethical principles of psychologists and code of conduct.

American Psychological Association (APA). (2015). Guidelines for psychological practice with transgender and gender nonconforming people. American Psychologist, 70(9), 832–864.

Bandura, A. (1999). Moral disengagement in the perpetration of inhumanities. *Personality and social psychology review*, *3*(3), 193-209.

Bandura, A., Barbaranelli, C., Caprara, G. V., &

Pastorelli, C. (1996). Mechanisms of moral disengagement in the exercise of moral agency. *Journal of personality and social psychology*, *71*(2), 364.

Bandura, A., Caprara, G. V., Barbaranelli, C., Pastorelli, C., & Regalia, C. (2001). Sociocognitive self-regulatory mechanisms governing transgressive behavior. *Journal of personality and social psychology*, *80*(1), 125.

Barsky, A. E. (2023). Essential ethics for social work practice. Oxford University Press.

Batson, C.D., Thompson, E.R. (2001). Why don't moral people act morally? Motivational considerations. Current Directions in Psychological Science, 10(2), 54–57.

Beauchamp, T. L., & Childress, J. F. (2019). Principles of biomedical ethics (8th ed). Oxford University Press.

Blasi, A. (1980). Bridging moral cognition and moral action: A critical review of the literature. *Psychological bulletin*, *88*(1), 1.

Bloom, P. (2010). The moral life of babies. *New York Times Magazine*, *3*, MM44.

Bloom, P., & Wynn, K. (2016). What develops in moral development. *Core knowledge and conceptual change*, 347-364.

Bostyn, D. H., & Roets, A. (2017). Trust, trolleys and social dilemmas: A replication study. *Journal of Experimental Psychology: General*, *146*(5), e1.

Branscombe, N. R., & Doosje, B. (Eds.). (2004). *Collective guilt: International perspectives.*

Cambridge University Press.

Brogaard, B. (2000). Hatred: Understanding Our Most Dangerous Emotion. Oxford University Press.

Brogaard, B. (2015). On Romantic Love. Oxford University Press.

Brown, M., & Sacco, D. F. (2019). Is pulling the lever sexy? Deontology as a downstream cue to long-term mate quality. *Journal of Social and Personal Relationships*, *36*(3), 957-976.

Bussey, K. (1999). Children's categorization and evaluation of different types of lies and truths. Child Development, 70(6), 1338–1347.

Cargill, J.R., and Curtis, D.A. (2017). Parental Deception: Perceived Effects on Parent-Child Relationships. Journal of Relationships Research, 8, e1.

Carlson, R. W., Bigman, Y. E., Gray, K., Ferguson, M. J., & Crockett, M. J. (2022). How inferred motives shape moral judgements. *Nature Reviews Psychology*, *1*(8), 468-478.

Case, C. R., & Maner, J. K. (2015). When and why power corrupts: An evolutionary perspective. In *Handbook on Evolution and Society* (pp. 460-473). Routledge.

Churchland, P. S. (2011). *Braintrust: What neuroscience tells us about morality*. Princeton University Press.

Cinelli, E. (2023, May 30). How Lying To Your Kids Can Impact Them As Adults. https://www.familyeducation.com › kids › values › how-lying-to-your-kids-can-impact-them-as-adults.

Cislak, A., Cichocka, A., Wojcik, A. D., & Frankowska, N. (2018). Power corrupts, but control does not: What stands behind the effects of holding high positions. *Personality and Social Psychology Bulletin*, *44*(6), 944-957.

Clay, R. (2023). Free speech vs. patient care: Psychologists are battling a growing trend that allows students to opt out of diversity training. Monitor on Psychology, 44(7).

Conway, P., & Gawronski, B. (2013). Deontological and utilitarian inclinations in moral decision making: a process dissociation approach. *Journal of personality and social psychology*, *104*(2), 216.

Cunningham, J. M. (n.d.). Did Marie-Antoinette really say "Let them eat cake?" Brittanica. Accessed 9th March 2024.

Curry, O. S. (2016). Morality as cooperation: a problem-centered approach. In The evolution of morality. T. K. Shackelford and R. D. Hansen, eds. Pp. 27–51. New York: Springer.

Curry, O. S., Chesters, M. J., & Van Lissa, C. J. (2019). Mapping morality with a compass: Testing the theory of 'morality-as-cooperation'with a new questionnaire. Journal of Research in Personality, 78, 106-124.

Dahl, A. (2014). Definitions and Developmental Processes in Research on Infant MoralityCommentary on Tafreshi, Thompson, and Racine. *Human Development*, *57*(4), 241-249.

De Waal, F. B., & Waal, F. D. (1996). *Good natured*. Harvard University Press.

DeCelles, K. A., DeRue, D. S., Margolis, J. D., & Ceranic, T. L. (2012). Does power corrupt or enable? When and why power facilitates self-interested behavior. *Journal of applied psychology*, *97*(3), 681.

DeScioli, P. (2016). The side-taking hypothesis for moral judgment. Current Opinion in Psychology, 7, 23-27.

Dunn, J. (2006). Moral development in early childhood and social interaction in the family. In: Killen, M., and Smetana, J.G., eds. (2006). Handbook of moral development, pp. 331-350. Mahwah, N.J.: Erlbaum

Eisenberg, N. (2000). Emotion, regulation, and moral development. *Annual review of psychology*, *51*(1), 665-697.

Ekman, P. (1989). The argument and evidence about universals in facial expressions. *Handbook of social psychophysiology*, *143*, 164.

Ekman, P. (1992). An argument for basic emotions. *Cognition & emotion*, *6*(3-4), 169-200.

Ellemers, N. (2017). *Morality and the regulation of social behavior: Groups as moral anchors*. Psychology Press.

Ellemers, N. (2018). Morality and social identity. *The Oxford handbook of the human essence*, 147-158.

Ellemers, N., & van den Bos, K. (2012). Morality

in groups: On the social-regulatory functions of right and wrong. *Social and Personality Psychology Compass*, *6*(12), 878-889.

Ellemers, N., & Van der Toorn, J. (2015). Groups as moral anchors. *Current Opinion in Psychology*, *6*, 189-194.

Ellemers, N., Van Der Toorn, J., Paunov, Y., & Van Leeuwen, T. (2019). The psychology of morality: A review and analysis of empirical studies published from 1940 through 2017. *Personality and Social Psychology Review*, *23*(4), 332-366.

Everett, J. A., Pizarro, D. A., & Crockett, M. J. (2016). Inference of trustworthiness from intuitive moral judgments. *Journal of Experimental Psychology: General*, *145*(6), 772.

Feinberg, M., Willer, R., Antonenko, O., & John, O. P. (2012). Liberating reason from the passions: Overriding intuitionist moral judgments through emotion reappraisal. *Psychological science*, *23*(7), 788-795.

Fiske, A. P. (1991). *Structures of social life: The four elementary forms of human relations: Communal sharing, authority ranking, equality matching, market pricing*. Free Press.

Fiske, A. P., Kitayama, S., Markus, H. R., & Nisbett, R. E. (1998). The cultural matrix of social psychology. In D. T. Gilbert, S. T. Fiske, & G. Lindzey (Eds.), *The handbook of social psychology* (4th ed., pp. 915–981). McGraw-Hill.

Fraser, B. (2012). The nature of moral judgements and the extent of the moral domain. *Philosophical Explorations*, *15*(1), 1-16.

Gawronski, B., Armstrong, J., Conway, P., Friesdorf, R., & Hütter, M. (2017). Consequences, norms, and generalized inaction in moral dilemmas: The CNI model of moral decision-making. *Journal of Personality and Social Psychology*, *113*(3), 343.

Giner-Sorolla, R., Kupfer, T., & Sabo, J. (2018). What makes moral disgust special? An integrative functional review. In *Advances in experimental social psychology* (Vol. 57, pp. 223-289). Academic Press.

Giurge, L. M., Van Dijke, M., Zheng, M. X., & De Cremer, D. (2021). Does power corrupt the mind? The influence of power on moral reasoning and self-interested behavior. *The Leadership Quarterly*, *32*(4), 101288.

Gleichgerrcht, E., & Young, L. (2013). Low levels of empathic concern predict utilitarian moral judgment. *PloS one*, *8*(4), e60418.

Gonser, S. (2023, Aug 24)). A parent's guide to lying and age-appropriate consequences. https://www.parents.com/kids/devel opment/behavioral/age-by-age-guide-to…

Graham, J., Haidt, J., & Nosek, B. A. (2009). Liberals and conservatives rely on different sets of moral foundations. Journal of Personality and Social Psychology, 96(5), 1029–1046.

Graham, J., Haidt, J., & Nosek, B. A. (2009). Liberals and conservatives rely on different sets of moral foundations. *Journal of personality and social psychology*, *96*(5), 1029.

Greene, J. (2013). Moral tribes: Emotion, reason, and the gap between us and them. Penguin.

Greene, J. (2014). *Moral tribes: Emotion, reason, and the gap between us and them.* Penguin.

Greene, J. D., Sommerville, R. B., Nystrom, L. E., Darley, J. M., & Cohen, J. D. (2001). An fMRI investigation of emotional engagement in moral judgment. *Science*, *293*(5537), 2105-2108.

Greene, J., & Haidt, J. (2002). How (and where) does moral judgment work?. *Trends in cognitive sciences*, *6*(12), 517-523.

Haidt, J. (2001). The emotional dog and its rational tail: a social intuitionist approach to moral judgment. *Psychological review*, *108*(4), 814.

Haidt, J. (2003). The moral emotions. *Handbook of affective sciences*, *11*(2003), 852-870.

Haidt, J. (2008). Morality. *Perspectives on psychological science*, *3*(1), 65-72.

Haidt, J. (2012). The righteous mind: Why good people are divided by politics and religion. Pantheon.

Haidt, J. (2012). *The righteous mind: Why good people are divided by politics and religion.* Vintage.

Haidt, J., & Hersh, M. A. (2001). Sexual morality: The cultures and emotions of conservatives and liberals 1. *Journal of Applied Social Psychology*, *31*(1), 191-221.

Haidt, J., Koller, S. H., & Dias, M. G. (1993). Affect, culture, and morality, or is it wrong to eat your dog?. *Journal of personality and social psychology*, *65*(4), 613.

Hamlin, J. K. (2015). Does the infant possess a

moral concept?.

Hamlin, J. K., & Wynn, K. (2011). Young infants prefer prosocial to antisocial others. *Cognitive development*, *26*(1), 30-39.

Hamlin, J. K., Mahajan, N., Liberman, Z., & Wynn, K. (2013). Not like me= bad: Infants prefer those who harm dissimilar others. *Psychological science*, *24*(4), 589-594.

Hamlin, J. K., Wynn, K., Bloom, P., & Mahajan, N. (2011). How infants and toddlers react to antisocial others. *Proceedings of the national academy of sciences*, *108*(50), 19931-19936.

Haslam, N., & Loughnan, S. (2014). Dehumanization and infrahumanization. *Annual review of psychology*, *65*, 399-423.

Heyman, G.D., Fu, G., and Lee, K. (2007). Evaluating claims people make about themselves: The development of skepticism. Child Development, 78(2), 367–375.

Hofmann, W., Wisneski, D. C., Brandt, M. J., & Skitka, L. J. (2014). Morality in everyday life. *Science*, *345*(6202), 1340-1343.

Howe, N. (2019). "Millennials and the loneliness epidemic." Forbes. May 3, 2019, "What young people fear the most," Viceland UK Census.

https://www.psychologytoday.com/us/blog/animal-emotions/201001/are-nonhuman-animals-more-moral-human-animals-yes-they-are

https://www.psychologytoday.com/us/blog/cutting-edge-leadership/202402/how-and-why-power-corrupts-people

https://www.psychologytoday.com/us/blog/experiments-in-philosophy/200806/do-atheists-pose-threat-morality

https://www.psychologytoday.com/us/blog/narcissism-demystified/202103/9-ways-many-narcissists-behave-cult-leaders

Human Rights Campaign. (n.d.). Map of state laws and policies.

Hume, D. (1773). Letter LXXI, dated 24th of March, 1773, in the Letters of David Hume to William Strahan. George Birkbeck Hill (ed.). Oxford: Clarendon Press (1888), 271.

Iceland, J., Silver, E., & Redstone, I. (2023). Why we disagree about inequality: Social Justice vs. Social Order. Polity Press.

Janoff-Bulman, R., & Carnes, N. C. (2013). Surveying the moral landscape: Moral motives and group-based moralities. *Personality and Social Psychology Review, 17*(3), 219-236.

Kagan, J. (2018). Three unresolved issues in human morality. *Perspectives on Psychological Science, 13*(3), 346-358.

Kohlberg, L. (1969). The cognitive-developmental approach to socialization. *Handbook of socialization theory and research. Chicago: Rand McNally*, 347-480.

Kohlberg, L. (1971). *Stages of moral development as a basis for moral education* (pp. 24-84). Cambridge: Center for Moral Education, Harvard University.

Kugler, M., Jost, J. T., & Noorbaloochi, S. (2014). Another look at moral foundations theory: Do authoritarianism and social dominance orientation explain liberal-conservative differences in "moral" intuitions?. *Social Justice Research*, *27*, 413-431.

Kupfer, T. R., & Giner-Sorolla, R. (2017). Communicating moral motives: The social signaling function of disgust. *Social Psychological and Personality Science*, *8*(6), 632-640.

Leach, C. W. (2017). Understanding shame and guilt. *Handbook of the psychology of self-forgiveness*, 17-28.

Leach, C. W., Ellemers, N., & Barreto, M. (2007). Group virtue: the importance of morality (vs. competence and sociability) in the positive evaluation of in-groups. *Journal of personality and social psychology*, *93*(2), 234.

Marshall, J., Wynn, K., & Bloom, P. (2020). Do children and adults take social relationship into account when evaluating people's actions?. *Child Development*, *91*(5), e1082-e1100.

McGowan, M. K. (2019). Just Words: On Speech and Hidden Harm. Oxford University Press.

Mill, J. S. (2016). Representative government. In *Democracy: A Reader* (pp. 58-66). Columbia University Press.

Monin, B., & Miller, D. T. (2001). Moral credentials and the expression of prejudice. *Journal of personality and social psychology*, *81*(1), 33.

Morales, M. (1997). The corrupting influence of power. In *Philosophical Perspectives on Power and*

Domination (pp. 41-53). Brill.

Morris, J. (1997). Care of empowerment? A disability rights perspective. *Social Policy & Administration, 31*(1), 54-60.

Moses, L.J., and Baldwin, D.A. (2005). What can the study of cognitive development reveal about children's ability to appreciate and cope with advertising? Journal of Public Policy and Marketing, 24(2), 186–201.

National Association of Social Workers. (2021). Code of ethics.

Perkins, S.A., and Turiel, E. (2007). To lie or not to lie: To whom and under what circumstances. Child Development, 78(2), 609–621.

Peterson, M. (2023). Ethics in the Gray Area. Cambridge, UK: Cambridge University Press.

Pismenny, A., Eickers, G., & Prinz, J. (2024). Emotional Injustice. Ergo: An Open Access Journal of Philosophy.

Pizarro, D. A., Uhlmann, E., & Bloom, P. (2003). Causal deviance and the attribution of moral responsibility. *Journal of experimental social psychology, 39*(6), 653-660.

Preuter, S., Jaeger, B., & Stel, M. (2023). The Costs Of Lying: Consequences Of Telling Lies On Liar's Self-Esteem And Affect. The British Journal Of Social Psychology, 10.1111/bjso.12711. Advance online publication.

Price, T. L. (2010). Understanding ethical failures in leadership. *Leading organizations: Perspectives for a new era*, 402-405.

Rai, T. S., & Fiske, A. P. (2011). Moral psychology is relationship regulation: moral motives for unity, hierarchy, equality, and proportionality. *Psychological review*, *118*(1), 57.

Rai, T. S., & Fiske, A. P. (2011). Moral psychology is relationship regulation: moral motives for unity, hierarchy, equality, and proportionality. *Psychological review*, *118*(1), 57.

Rest, J. R. (1984). Research on moral development: Implications for training counseling psychologists. *The Counseling Psychologist*, *12*(3), 19-29.

Rozin, P., Lowery, L., Imada, S., & Haidt, J. (1999). The CAD triad hypothesis: a mapping between three moral emotions (contempt, anger, disgust) and three moral codes (community, autonomy, divinity). *Journal of personality and social psychology*, *76*(4), 574.

Russell, P. S., & Giner-Sorolla, R. (2013). Bodily moral disgust: what it is, how it is different from anger, and why it is an unreasoned emotion. *Psychological bulletin*, *139*(2), 328.

Sacco, D. F., Brown, M., Lustgraaf, C. J., & Hugenberg, K. (2017). The adaptive utility of deontology: Deontological moral decision-making fosters perceptions of trust and likeability. *Evolutionary Psychological Science*, *3*, 125-132.

Sacks, J. (2020). Morality: Restoring the common good in divided times. New York, NY: Basic Books.

Saltzstein, H. D., & Kasachkoff, T. (2004).

Haidt's moral intuitionist theory: A psychological and philosophical critique. *Review of general psychology*, *8*(4), 273-282.

Šamánková, D., Preiss, M., Příhodová, T., Šamánková, D., Preiss, M., & Příhodová, T. (2018). Evolution of moral sense and moral judgement. *The Contextual Character of Moral Integrity: Transcultural Psychological Applications*, 59-75.

Schnall, S., Haidt, J., Clore, G. L., & Jordan, A. H. (2008). Disgust as embodied moral judgment. *Personality and social psychology bulletin*, *34*(8), 1096-1109.

Seiter, J.S., Bruschke, J., and Bai, C. (2002). The acceptability of deception as a function of perceivers' culture, deceiver's intention and deceiver-deceived relationship. Western Journal of Communication, 66(2), 158–180.

Seltzer, L.F. (2013, Apr 30). A new take on manipulation. https://www.psychologytoday.com/us/blog/evolution-the-self/201304/new-t...

Seltzer, L.F. (2019,Sep 25). How white are your white lies? https://www.psychologytoday.com/us/blog/evolution-the-self/201909/how-w...

Seltzer, L.F. (2022, Aug 17). When truth is overrated: The advantages of dishonesty. https://www.psychologytoday.com/us/blog/evolution-the-self/202208/when-...

Setoh, P., Zhao, S., Santos, R., Heyman, G.D., and Lee, K. (2020). Parenting by lying in childhood is associated with negative developmental outcomes in adulthood. Journal of Experimental Child Psychology, 189, 104680.

Sheikh, S. (2014). Cultural variations in shame's responses: A dynamic perspective. *Personality and Social Psychology Review, 18*(4), 387-403.

Sheikh, S., & Janoff-Bulman, R. (2010). The "shoulds" and "should nots" of moral emotions: A self-regulatory perspective on shame and guilt. *Personality and social psychology bulletin, 36*(2), 213-224.

Sheskin, M., Bloom, P., & Wynn, K. (2014). Anti-equality: Social comparison in young children. *Cognition, 130*(2), 152-156.

Skitka, L. J. (2010). The psychology of moral conviction. *Social and Personality Psychology Compass, 4*(4), 267-281.

Skitka, L. J., & Bauman, C. W. (2008). Moral conviction and political engagement. *Political Psychology, 29*(1), 29-54.

Skitka, L. J., & Mullen, E. (2002). Understanding judgments of fairness in a real-world political context: A test of the value protection model of justice reasoning. *Personality and Social Psychology Bulletin, 28*(10), 1419-1429.

Skitka, L. J., Bauman, C. W., & Sargis, E. G. (2005). Moral conviction: Another contributor to attitude strength or something more?. *Journal of personality and social psychology, 88*(6), 895.

Sutton, R., & Douglas, K. (2019). *Social psychology*.

Bloomsbury Publishing.

Talwar, V. (2022, Jul). The truth about why kids lie. https://www.apa.org/news/podcasts/speaking-of-psychology/why-kids-lie

Tan, C. (2020) "Mindfulness and morality: educational insights from Confucius." Journal of Moral Education.

Tangney, J. P., & Dearing, R. L. (2003). *Shame and guilt*. Guilford press.

Tangney, J. P., Miller, R. S., Flicker, L., & Barlow, D. H. (1996). Are shame, guilt, and embarrassment distinct emotions?. *Journal of personality and social psychology*, *70*(6), 1256.

Tangney, J. P., Stuewig, J., & Martinez, A. G. (2014). Two faces of shame: The roles of shame and guilt in predicting recidivism. *Psychological science*, *25*(3), 799-805.

Tangney, J. P., Stuewig, J., & Mashek, D. J. (2007). Moral emotions and moral behavior. *Annu. Rev. Psychol.*, *58*, 345-372.

Tangney, J. P., Wagner, P. E., Hill-Barlow, D., Marschall, D. E., & Gramzow, R. (1996). Relation of shame and guilt to constructive versus destructive responses to anger across the lifespan. *Journal of personality and social psychology*, *70*(4), 797.

Tapp, C., & Occhipinti, S. (2016). The essence of crime: Contagious transmission from those who have committed moral transgressions. *British journal of social psychology*, *55*(4), 756-772.

Tetlock, P. E. (2003). Thinking the unthinkable:

Sacred values and taboo cognitions. *Trends in cognitive sciences*, *7*(7), 320-324.

Tobiáš, T. S. (2020). *What could be a model that combines the evolution of morality through natural selection with the way we make moral judgements shaped by culturally evolved morality?* (Doctoral dissertation, Ludwig Maximilians University of Munich).

Tomasello, M., & Vaish, A. (2013). Origins of human cooperation and morality. *Annual review of psychology*, *64*, 231-255.

Turiel, E. (2006). Thought, emotions, and social interactional processes in moral development. *Handbook of moral development*, *2*.

Turiel, E. (2006). Thought, emotions, and social interactional processes in moral development. *Handbook of moral development*, *2*.

United States Constitution, First Amendment. (1791).

Ward v. Polite. (2012). No. 09-11237 (US. Court of Appeals).

Waytz, A., and W. Hofmann. (2019). "Nudging the better angels of our nature: a field experiment on morality and well-being." Emotion. 20(5). pp. 904-909.

Wertz, S. K. (2018). Little White Lies. International Journal of Applied Philosophy, 32(1), 49-55.

Whiteley, C (2022) *Cult Psychology: A Guide To The Personality, Social Psychology, Cognitive and Forensic Psychology of Cults*, CGD Publishing, England

Whiteley, C. (2022) Psychology of Relationships: The Social Psychology of Friendships, Romantic Relationships and More. CGD Publishing. England.

Whiteley, C. (2022) Psychology of Relationships: The Social Psychology of Friendships, Romantic Relationships, Prosocial Behaviour and More. CGD Publishing. England.

Whiteley, C. (2022) Social Psychology: A Guide to Social and Cultural Psychology. CGD Publishing England.

Wright, J.C. (in press). Diversity, deviance, and virtue within imperfect moral communities. Virtues and Virtue Education: Local or Universal? Routledge Press.

Wynn, K., & Bloom, P. (2014). The moral baby. In M. Killen & J. G. Smetana (Eds.), *Handbook of moral development* (2nd ed., pp. 435–453). Psychology Press.

Wynn, K., Bloom, P., Jordan, A., Marshall, J., & Sheskin, M. (2018). Not noble savages after all: Limits to early altruism. *Current Directions in Psychological Science*, *27*(1), 3-8.

Zhong, C. B., & Liljenquist, K. (2006). Washing away your sins: Threatened morality and physical cleansing. *Science*, *313*(5792), 1451-1452.

https://www.subscribepage.io/psychologyboxset

CHECK OUT THE PSYCHOLOGY WORLD PODCAST FOR MORE PSYCHOLOGY INFORMATION! AVAILABLE ON ALL MAJOR PODCAST APPS.

About the author:

Connor Whiteley is the author of over 60 books in the sci-fi fantasy, nonfiction psychology and books for writer's genre and he is a Human Branding Speaker and Consultant.

He is a passionate warhammer 40,000 reader, psychology student and author.

Who narrates his own audiobooks and he hosts The Psychology World Podcast.

All whilst studying Psychology at the University of Kent, England.

Also, he was a former Explorer Scout where he gave a speech to the Maltese President in August 2018 and he attended Prince Charles' 70th Birthday Party at Buckingham Palace in May 2018.

Plus, he is a self-confessed coffee lover!

Other books by Connor Whiteley:
Bettie English Private Eye Series
A Very Private Woman
The Russian Case
A Very Urgent Matter
A Case Most Personal
Trains, Scots and Private Eyes
The Federation Protects
Cops, Robbers and Private Eyes
Just Ask Bettie English
An Inheritance To Die For
The Death of Graham Adams
Bearing Witness
The Twelve
The Wrong Body
The Assassination Of Bettie English
Wining And Dying
Eight Hours
Uniformed Cabal
A Case Most Christmas

Gay Romance Novellas
Breaking, Nursing, Repairing A Broken Heart
Jacob And Daniel
Fallen For A Lie
Spying And Weddings
Clean Break

MORAL PSYCHOLOGY

Awakening Love
Meeting A Country Man
Loving Prime Minister
Snowed In Love
Never Been Kissed
Love Betrays You

<u>Lord of War Origin Trilogy:</u>
Not Scared Of The Dark
Madness
Burn Them All

<u>Way Of The Odyssey</u>
Odyssey of Rebirth
Convergence of Odysseys

<u>Lady Tano Fantasy Adventure Stories</u>
Betrayal
Murder
Annihilation

<u>The Fireheart Fantasy Series</u>
Heart of Fire
Heart of Lies
Heart of Prophecy
Heart of Bones
Heart of Fate

City of Assassins (Urban Fantasy)
City of Death
City of Martyrs
City of Pleasure
City of Power

Agents of The Emperor
Return of The Ancient Ones
Vigilance
Angels of Fire
Kingmaker
The Eight
The Lost Generation
Hunt
Emperor's Council
Speaker of Treachery
Birth Of The Empire
Terraforma
Spaceguard

The Rising Augusta Fantasy Adventure Series
Rise To Power
Rising Walls
Rising Force
Rising Realm

<u>Lord Of War Trilogy (Agents of The Emperor)</u>
Not Scared Of The Dark
Madness
Burn It All Down

<u>Miscellaneous:</u>
RETURN
FREEDOM
SALVATION
Reflection of Mount Flame
The Masked One
The Great Deer
English Independence

OTHER SHORT STORIES BY CONNOR WHITELEY

<u>Mystery Short Story Collections</u>
Criminally Good Stories Volume 1: 20 Detective Mystery Short Stories
Criminally Good Stories Volume 2: 20 Private Investigator Short Stories
Criminally Good Stories Volume 3: 20 Crime Fiction Short Stories
Criminally Good Stories Volume 4: 20 Science Fiction and Fantasy Mystery Short

Stories
Criminally Good Stories Volume 5: 20 Romantic Suspense Short Stories

Connor Whiteley Starter Collections:
Agents of The Emperor Starter Collection
Bettie English Starter Collection
Matilda Plum Starter Collection
Gay Romance Starter Collection
Way Of The Odyssey Starter Collection
Kendra Detective Fiction Starter Collection

Mystery Short Stories:
Protecting The Woman She Hated
Finding A Royal Friend
Our Woman In Paris
Corrupt Driving
A Prime Assassination
Jubilee Thief
Jubilee, Terror, Celebrations
Negative Jubilation
Ghostly Jubilation
Killing For Womenkind
A Snowy Death
Miracle Of Death
A Spy In Rome
The 12:30 To St Pancreas

A Country In Trouble
A Smokey Way To Go
A Spicy Way To GO
A Marketing Way To Go
A Missing Way To Go
A Showering Way To Go
Poison In The Candy Cane
Kendra Detective Mystery Collection Volume 1
Kendra Detective Mystery Collection Volume 2
Mystery Short Story Collection Volume 1
Mystery Short Story Collection Volume 2
Criminal Performance
Candy Detectives
Key To Birth In The Past

<u>Science Fiction Short Stories:</u>
Their Brave New World
Gummy Bear Detective
The Candy Detective
What Candies Fear
The Blurred Image
Shattered Legions
The First Rememberer
Life of A Rememberer
System of Wonder

Lifesaver
Remarkable Way She Died
The Interrogation of Annabella Stormic
Blade of The Emperor
Arbiter's Truth
Computation of Battle
Old One's Wrath
Puppets and Masters
Ship of Plague
Interrogation
Edge of Failure

<u>Fantasy Short Stories:</u>
City of Snow
City of Light
City of Vengeance
Dragons, Goats and Kingdom
Smog The Pathetic Dragon
Don't Go In The Shed
The Tomato Saver
The Remarkable Way She Died
Dragon Coins
Dragon Tea
Dragon Rider

MORAL PSYCHOLOGY

All books in 'An Introductory Series':
Clinical Psychology and Transgender Clients
Clinical Psychology
Careers In Psychology
Psychology of Suicide
Dementia Psychology
Clinical Psychology Reflections Volume 4
Forensic Psychology of Terrorism And Hostage-Taking
Forensic Psychology of False Allegations
Year In Psychology
CBT For Anxiety
CBT For Depression
Applied Psychology
BIOLOGICAL PSYCHOLOGY 3RD EDITION
COGNITIVE PSYCHOLOGY THIRD EDITION
SOCIAL PSYCHOLOGY- 3RD EDITION
ABNORMAL PSYCHOLOGY 3RD EDITION
PSYCHOLOGY OF RELATIONSHIPS- 3RD EDITION
DEVELOPMENTAL PSYCHOLOGY 3RD EDITION
HEALTH PSYCHOLOGY
RESEARCH IN PSYCHOLOGY

CONNOR WHITELEY

A GUIDE TO MENTAL HEALTH AND TREATMENT AROUND THE WORLD- A GLOBAL LOOK AT DEPRESSION
FORENSIC PSYCHOLOGY
THE FORENSIC PSYCHOLOGY OF THEFT, BURGLARY AND OTHER CRIMES AGAINST PROPERTY
CRIMINAL PROFILING: A FORENSIC PSYCHOLOGY GUIDE TO FBI PROFILING AND GEOGRAPHICAL AND STATISTICAL PROFILING.
CLINICAL PSYCHOLOGY
FORMULATION IN PSYCHOTHERAPY
PERSONALITY PSYCHOLOGY AND INDIVIDUAL DIFFERENCES
CLINICAL PSYCHOLOGY REFLECTIONS VOLUME 1
CLINICAL PSYCHOLOGY REFLECTIONS VOLUME 2
Clinical Psychology Reflections Volume 3
CULT PSYCHOLOGY
Police Psychology

www.ingramcontent.com/pod-product-compliance
Ingram Content Group UK Ltd.
Pitfield, Milton Keynes, MK11 3LW, UK
UKHW030648130225
455042UK00007B/42